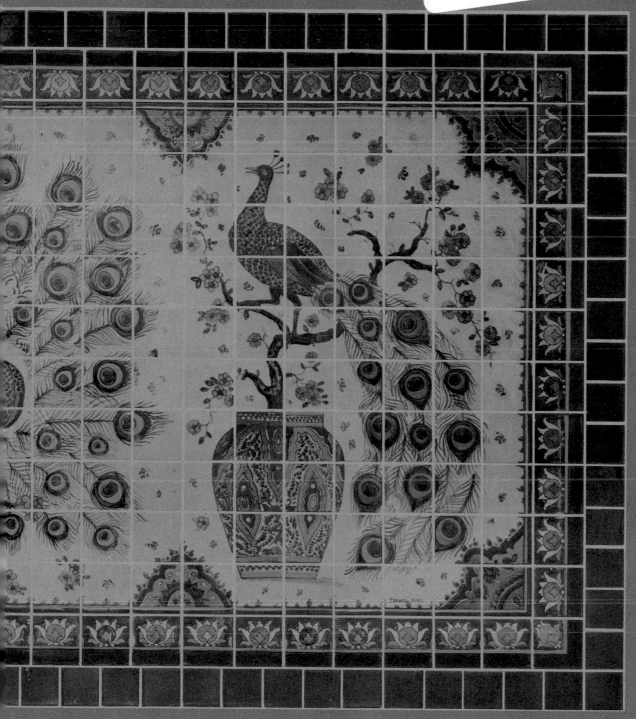

MARION KOOGLER McNAY
A Biography
1883-1950

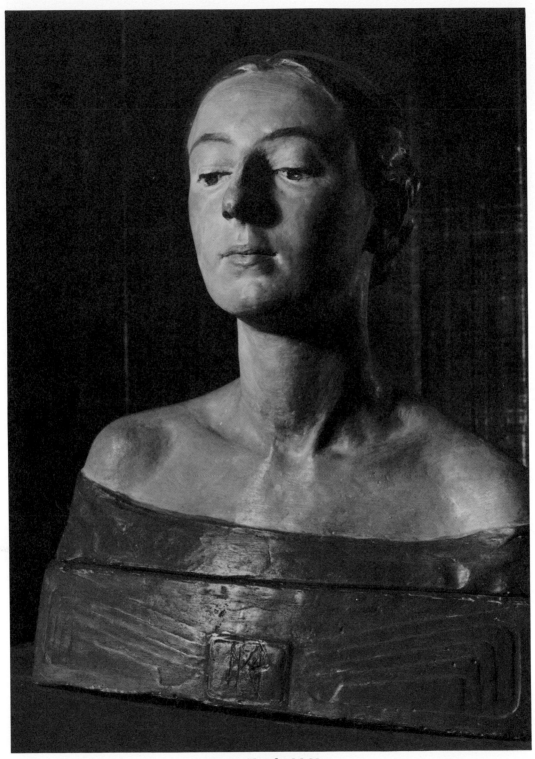

Marion Koogler McNay
Artist unknown, polychrome and plaster
Collection, Marion Koogler McNay Art Institute

MARION KOOGLER McNAY

A Biography

1883 - 1950

by

Lois Wood Burkhalter

Published by the

MARION KOOGLER McNAY
ART INSTITUTE

A MUSEUM OF MODERN ART

San Antonio, Texas

INTRODUCTION

On April 13, 1950, the newspapers of San Antonio, Texas, announced the death of Mrs. Marion Koogler McNay, sixty-seven years of age. The obituaries identified her as a philanthropist and patron of the arts but were otherwise and noticeably lacking in biographical details. Other information contained in the news stories, however, was of more than ordinary interest. For the first time the people of San Antonio learned that Mrs. McNay's superb collection of modern art, her impressive home, and a large and perpetual endowment were left in trust for the use and enjoyment of her adopted city. It was the largest single public gift in the city's history.

The donor was almost a stranger to the general public, known only to a comparatively small circle of artists and art patrons. The public was equally unfamiliar with Mrs. McNay's collection of modern French art. During the four-year interval between Mrs. McNay's death and the opening of the Marion Koogler McNay Art Institute the donor continued to remain a somewhat mysterious stranger who had built a home of great beauty and filled it with art treasures of her own discriminating selection.

San Antonio became aware of the full potentiality of the bequest and the opportunity it afforded for the promotion of the city's cultural growth when the Marion Koogler McNay Art Institute opened to the public on November 4, 1954. Mrs. McNay's home of architectural rarity, her gardens of careful planning, and her notable collection of modern European and American art were now in the public domain and privately administered by a board of trustees which Mrs. McNay had named in her will.

The functions of a museum and its scope of interest and meaning are not, of course, restricted to one community but are immeasurably and constantly extended to an ever-widening sphere of influence. Such a bequest soon becomes national wealth as well as a community asset. Invariably, visitors to the Institute, and particularly those from European art centers, express amazement at finding such a richness of modern French art in Texas, a state often erroneously prejudged as being in a cultural drouth of long duration. The key to this apparent anomaly obviously was the woman who founded the Museum.

Who was this woman whose munificent public gift had been assembled with such infallible taste and so quietly that only a few had been aware of its existence? Who was she whose personal taste, now displayed to the public in tangible form, had established a jewel of a museum of the highest standards which would have a timeless influence on the intellectual life of a wide community? What *kind* of woman was she? What was the source of personal means which permitted this visible evidence of her feeling and love for beauty and her knowledge of art?

This biography attempts to answer these and other questions which are repeatedly asked by Museum visitors and proposes to present in a small measure the private life of a woman whose former possessions are now a public privilege.

Primarily, however, this biography is intended to be the biography of a museum, a museum conceived, planned, and perpetuated in the final years of the life of Marion Koogler McNay. All the years before and their events were but preliminaries directed toward this singular achievement.

Viewed through the eyes of a widely divergent group who knew Marion Koogler McNay, she was a person of contrasting characteristics, truly a many-faceted woman. But all agree that in the fulfillment of the deed which set her apart Mrs. McNay followed her own judgment and taste and never deviated from her goal.

Marion Koogler McNay's remarkable will, which covers the minutest of possible contingencies and assures the preservation and continuation of her impeccable taste, further attests her dedication. Plans for the conversion of her home into a public art museum were accomplished in the last few years of her life when chronic illness caused her to live in reclusive splendor in her mansion at Sunset Hills.

Indeed, this complex woman did not initiate plans for her eventual benefaction until she was fifty-nine years old and her personal life consigned to sometimes painful memory. In a comparatively brief period of eight years Marion Koogler McNay fulfilled her self-appointed destiny with such fidelity that John P. Leeper, the director under whose guidance her dream of a museum was to become a reality, expressed not only his own but the appreciation of the public when he wrote:

"A profound debt of gratitude is owed Marion Koogler McNay, a debt best repaid by maintaining the severe standards of quality which governed her taste in paint-

ing, by seeking the young, the vital, and the experimental, by using and enjoying her collection with the same unswerving intelligence with which it was formed and given to the people."

The proposal for a biography of the founder of the Marion Koogler McNay Art Institute originated with Mrs. H. Lutcher Brown who served as president of the Board of Trustees during the first twelve years of the Museum's existence and who was intimately associated with Marion Koogler McNay in the operation of the San Antonio Art Institute and during the time the Museum Collection was being assembled.

Mrs. Brown's belief that a biography should not be left to another generation was particularly pertinent because of the void of personal papers. The facts of Marion Koogler McNay's life existed largely in the memories of living persons and these original sources for research and data were, at the most, ephemeral.

I was greatly honored by the assignment to write the biography. Its completion was made possible only through the constant cooperation of the three board members who constituted a committee-in-charge: Mrs. Brown, Mrs. Ellen S. Quillin, and Mrs. Fleet S. (Elsie Whitney) McNay. I should like to acknowledge my deep appreciation to them and also to Mrs. Ruth Hatfield of Los Angeles, to Mrs. Gladys Teter Spencer of El Dorado, Kansas, to Mrs. Gilard Kargl, art consultant, and to the many others whose memories and contributions constitute the text of this biography.

Lois Wood Burkhalter

Jacket and book design by Ben Carlton Mead

CONTENTS

ILLUSTRATIONS

MARION KOOGLER McNAY
A Biography
1883-1950

I. THE EARLY YEARS

The bustle on Sunset Hills that fall in 1927 created more than passing interest among the people of San Antonio, Texas. A house of impressive proportions was going up on the caliche hill of the old Gonfacio Rodríquez farm out on the Austin Highway and it was said that the doctor's new wife, a wealthy widow from Ohio, was building a mansion to replace the little farmhouse which had occupied the hill for as far back as anyone could remember.

Few of the neighbors had met the attractive bride of Dr. Donald Taylor Atkinson and most would not until the house was finished. For the present, she was much too occupied to be neighborly.

The house had emerged slowly from the initial planning shortly after Marion Koogler and Dr. Atkinson were married on May 12, 1926, in Austin, Texas. Dr. Atkinson wanted, so he told his wife, the finest house in San Antonio and in this she was in accord. He also wanted to make an extended tour of Europe and the Near East but in this his wife demurred. Europe could wait until the house was finished.

Presently she was standing on a nine-foot ladder stenciling the ceiling of the dining room. She wore faded blue dungarees only a little more paint-stained than her face and hands.

Below and around her, plasterers and painters worked at their crafts only occasionally aware of the presence of the small woman on the ladder. She had designed and cut the stencils and would not entrust to anyone else the tedious process of applying them to ceiling and archway facings. Marion Koogler McNay was creating her masterpiece, which was to endure as the tangible consummation of her long years in the study of the visual arts.

Meanwhile, the Atkinsons lived in the little farmhouse and raised pedigreed Nubian goats, peacocks, and Irish terriers. Unlike Mrs. Isabela Stewart Gardner who created a Venetian palace in Boston and left it as a museum, Marion Koogler did not find it necessary to bring her lunch while supervising construction of her home. The farmhouse in which she lived was only a few yards away and from it she could keep a critical eye on building activities.

The architectural style of the house was loosely termed "Mediterranean" but closely followed the Spanish tradition for which San Antonio's sub-tropical climate and plants and its historic background offered an harmonious setting. Her long acquaintance with colonial Spanish architecture began in Laredo, Texas, and later developed in Florida with the more pretentious Ponce de Leon Hotel in San Augustine and the fortress-like Hotel Rolyat in St. Petersburg.

In the 1920's San Antonio's Spanish and Mexican origins and traditions could not only be found in a few crumbling survivors of the pre-revolutionary era but in modern versions as private homes, public buildings, schools, churches, and even filling stations. The guiding influence behind this regional renaissance were Atlee B. Ayres and his son Robert M. Ayres, both of them scholars of Spanish and Mexican architecture and art.

The Ayreses possessed the imagination and vision to create her perfect house and after months of research and critical study of plans of outstanding examples of Spanish-inspired homes in the United

States, the Atkinson residence reached the blueprint stage, but only after each detail had been approved by Marion Koogler. The architects were frequently astonished and impressed by her flair for style, her accuracy of scale planning, her suggestions and insistence on small accents, and her general knowledge of technical problems. Out of this association grew a long and sincere friendship of mutual admiration.

Construction began in August, 1927, with George W. Mitchell, Sr., as general contractor. The house, considered to be the finest in the city up to that time, was completed sixteen months later but the over-all project of out-buildings, additional patios, walks, gardens, and other details required three years. Total construction cost was about $250,000; duplication cost today would be closer to $800,000.

In the construction of her house Marion Koogler, ordinarily a prudent woman in money matters, showed none of the frugality which her father throughout his life had constantly urged her to practice. She could well afford to be extravagant, for now, since the recent death of her mother, she was the sole heir to a seemingly inexhaustible oil fortune from her late father's Kansas land.

Additionally, if her inherent thriftiness was occasionally shocked by her prodigality, she recalled her only home other than her parental one. It had been little more than a *jacal* in Laredo. That was long ago, but never too far away not to rush back with the force of a tidal wave and engulf her in unbearable nostalgia.

On Sunset Hills Marion Koogler McNay was building a new home and a new life with a husband so like her revered father that a good life seemed assured despite her now and then reversion to her old role of a sometime capricious daughter. Now, at forty-three years of age, Marion Koogler for the first time in her life was independent, both financially and parentally, but the powerful influence of her father was far too enduring to rest with his ashes.

For most of those forty-three years she had lived under the watchful eye of her doting parents and was as adored, spoiled, and indulged as she had been when she was born, the only child of Dr. Marion A. and Clara (Lippincott) Koogler.

Her birth on February 7, 1883, in DeGraff, Logan County, Ohio, came ten years after the marriage of her parents. She was christened Jessie Marion in honor of her father and an aunt and was called Jessie until she discarded that in favor of her father's name.

Dr. Koogler came from a family of Ohio farmers and was the first of the family to forsake farming for a profession. The shortage of doctors and hospitals during the Civil War, in which he served with the Union Army although he was only sixteen years of age, influenced him to enter Jefferson Medical College. After graduating Dr. Koogler settled in DeGraff and although he practiced for almost forty years the respect for good farm land was so deeply ingrained that his profession served only as a means by which to acquire it. Dr. Koogler was twenty-five years old when on April 20, 1873, he married Clara Lippincott, the twenty-one-year-old daughter of the Andrew Jackson Lippincotts of DeGraff.

The Lippincott family had a proud heritage and was among the earliest Ohio settlers. Three of Clara Lippincott's ancestors fought in the American Revolution and one was captain of a spy company under General William Henry Harrison in the War of 1812. Another had contributed to early Americana by weaving a blue and white coverlet signed "Lippincott, Lima, Ohio," which the family carefully preserved and which later inspired the collection of early American textiles now in the Marion Koogler McNay Art Institute.

When Jessie was a year old her father made a difficult decision to leave a comfortable practice, lifelong friends, and relatives to move to El Dorado, Kansas,

The Koogler home in El Dorado, Kansas, where Marion Koogler spent her early years

to become doctor and surgeon for the Santa Fe Railroad. Particularly was it an unhappy decision for Mrs. Koogler who reluctantly parted with the clannish Lippincotts and the town in which she was born, where her social position was firmly and traditionally assured. In El Dorado, where even today one's status is often determined by the year of migration, she would be just another "newcomer."

El Dorado, in 1884 a thriving township, had long since lost its frontier character and was mellowing in gentility. Some of the community's pioneers had been there since territorial days and others, veterans of the Grand Army of the Republic, had selected their service bonuses of one hundred sixty acres in the valley of the Walnut River.

In this environment Jessie grew up but it can hardly be said that she matured. Personality traits which were indicated at an early age would intensify in the years ahead: complete dependence on her father, an impulsive generosity, an unexpected sense of humor in one so deeply introverted, and a tendency to take to her bed when events and people went against her will. Jessie was smothered in parental love and protected to the extent that even the natural act of learning to walk was an individual independence postponed beyond the average age.

The same environment also gave Marion Koogler in her later years her earthiness and humor, her loyalty, her love for nature and, in some unaccountable way, her devotion to art and beauty.

3

Dr. Koogler, holding his daughter's hand or never letting her out of his sight as they walked past the sturdy limestone buildings of El Dorado's main street, was soon a familiar figure in the town. Together they attended functions at Ellet's Opera House which opened two years before the Kooglers arrived. Traveling theatrical companies, taking advantage of the low rail fares to El Dorado, frequently appeared at the Opera House and when professionals were lacking, home talent took over the stage.

The Kooglers found the town agreeable enough, but Mrs. Koogler pined for Ohio. Their first home was a modest frame house at 608 Starr Street, still in use and renumbered 620. In addition to his service with the railroad, Dr. Koogler practiced in partnership with Dr. W. F. Kuhn and after his death with Dr. R. S. Miller. From the beginning he was successful and soon acquired a reputation as a surgeon of unusual skill. The town's most prominent citizens were numbered among his patients.

Jessie frequently accompanied Dr. Koogler on his social and business calls. She was long to remember her visits to the imposing dark red house of the Murdocks. Thomas Benton Murdock, the political boss of Butler County who wore Brooks Brothers suits and whose sartorial elegance later was a contributing factor in his political downfall, was also owner of the El Dorado *Republican*. His wife was the talented Mrs. Marie Antoinette Murdock who taught elocution and who reviewed books for her husband's newspaper. Her every-day dramatics and her great zest for life were admired and imitated by little Jessie whose late developing verve and histrionics were reminiscent of the remarkable Mrs. Murdock.

Another woman who influenced the later-day Jessie was Mrs. Fannie DeGrasse Black, a singer from Wisconsin who was the leading talent scout for the endless list of light operas which she directed. Miss DeGrasse had appeared in El Dorado in 1873 under the auspices of the local Beethoven Club and remained in the town as the wife of the club's president, Judge Samuel Edward Black. Fannie Black was the undisputed queen of El Dorado's social life and ruled it for forty years.

When Jessie was nine years old, the Kooglers moved into a more pretentious house, a two-story white frame one which Judge Volney P. Mooney had built in 1886 at 729 West Central Avenue. The house is still in use and in good repair although lacking its original lovely gingerbread porch railings and quaint ornamentations.

Despite the fact that the new neighborhood was more fashionable and the neighbors were the most prosperous and influential in El Dorado, the Kooglers maintained their watchful supervision of Jessie's activities. She was never permitted to join in sidewalk games, nor to go swimming in Walnut Creek on a hot summer day, nor to ride horseback across the surrounding prairies. The Kooglers' Jessie remained indoors reading, drawing, or daydreaming in a secret world.

But as a medical man Dr. Koogler came to realize that Jessie's indoor life in her own private play world was a contributing factor to her delicate health and frequent illnesses. For this reason he prescribed exercise and bought Jessie a pony despite Clara Koogler's certainty that her beloved daughter would be killed in a fall. He hired a neighborhood girl to saddle the pony— a chore the other youngsters always did for themselves as part of the sport—and arranged for private riding lessons. Jessie on her little pony soon was trailing the other girls on their fast horses. As a concession to the worried Mrs. Koogler, the entire cavalcade periodically circled the block to wave reassuringly to Mrs. Koogler that Jessie still held her seat.

To placate Mrs. Koogler over the purchase of the pony, the doctor bought a piano and sent Jessie to the formidable Mrs. Fannie DeGrasse Black for lessons. She also had a weekly class in elocution, a part of every genteel young lady's education, with Mrs. Murdock. Jessie showed more talent in elocution than in music and once overcame her extreme shyness and gave a reading of *Entertaining Sister's Beau* at a church social at the home of her friend Corah Mooney.

Mrs. Corah Mooney Bullock still lives in the house her father built when the Kooglers moved into the old Mooney home. As was her father, she is the leading spirit in the Butler County Historical Society. As historian of the First Baptist Church of El Dorado, Mrs. Bullock recalled that Clara Koogler had been a member and church organist. Jessie attended the church as a child but when Dr. Koogler joined the Presbyterian Church she followed him. In time, Corah Mooney succeeded Mrs. Black as the entrepreneur of local talent and she once cast Jessie Koogler in the leading role of *Hamlet,* which she enacted with such unexpected vigor that the Mooneys' antique table was considerably endangered by an impromptu leap onto its top. Another time, selecting a cast for *Gypsy Encampment* and remembering Jessie's dramatization, Corah assigned her to an insignificant role. But again Corah underestimated her and the minor character emerged as a major one as interpreted and performed by Jessie. More than half a century later, the bright and bird-like Corah Mooney Bullock recalled: "I *must* say, Jessie thoroughly overdid it again."

Although music and drama had long been a part of the social and cultural life of El Dorado, pictorial art was non-existent. Ironically, the town offered an exceedingly barren breeding ground for such artistic discernment as Marion Koogler was later to show. But somehow the seed was there in the El Dorado of her girlhood.

At an early age Jessie began to express herself in painting and apparently without instruction since none was available in El Dorado. But painting was a part of her childhood secret world and today no one in El Dorado remembers that she had any interest in art until she entered college.

Extant are two small oil paintings on cardboard, both dated and signed on the back: "June, 1892, El Dorado, Kansas, Jessie M. Koogler." One is a painting of sailboats on a lake, the other of a fisherman launching a canoe. They reveal an unbelievable degree of maturity and a skill far beyond that of the average nine-year-old child. She never parted with these early beginnings and it is doubtful that she ever parted with any other drawings or paintings of her own. Although she was generous with works of other artists, Marion Koogler was never known to distribute her efforts among friends and relatives who would have cherished them. When she died the work of her lifetime was intact.

Jessie saw her first art exhibit when she was ten years old. That was in Chicago at the World's Columbian Exposition in 1893. Unknowingly, Marion Koogler witnessed the first open rebellion in the United States against the conventional dictates of the French salon. The heretics had been arbitrarily slipped into vacant spaces by their leading exponent in Chicago, Mrs. Potter Palmer, but their presence scarcely ruffled the two hundred thousand square feet of heroic realism. Jessie carried a catalogue of the exhibition back to El Dorado and kept it all the rest of her life.

Less than a year after Dr. Koogler arrived in El Dorado he made his first Butler County land purchase of eighty acres for which he paid less than nine dollars an acre. With a farmer's appreciation for hardy nature, he sought out lands on which grew the durable and nutritious native grass called bluestem which with great determination to survive clings to the soil where nature planted it and extends its roots as far under the earth as eleven feet. When Dr. Koogler began buying up Butler County land he consulted James W. Teter, one of his close friends and patients. Teter was the son-in-law of Ole Erickson Ladd, a native of Norway, who recognized the value of bluestem in 1858. Their descendants today lease the same land for grazing, and Texas Herefords and Angus now fatten on

5

Fisherman, oil on board, painted by Marion Koogler at the age of nine; McNay Art Institute archives

the same stand of bluestem which the ravenous Longhorns of another day failed to damage.

Dr. Koogler's thirst for acquiring bluestem land never diminished and by exercising middlewest frugality, buying up mortgages, attending sheriff's sales, and taking advantage of a bargain, he added acre after acre to his holdings. By 1908 he owned three thousand, two hundred and forty-eight acres, all in Butler County and southwest of El Dorado. His acquisitiveness was to prove immeasurably beneficial to future generations although it failed to add materially to the personal happiness of his family.

As Jessie grew older her parents became even more restrictive and she even more docile and obedient. Some of the neighbors thought their aloofness was nothing more than small-town snobbery but one thing was apparent to all: Dr. Koogler thought none of the boys around El Dorado was good enough for his Jessie.

She had few chances to meet young men. During high school she was rarely allowed to have dates and absolutely forbidden to attend dances or to join any of the social groups such as the Pastime Club to which most of her schoolmates belonged. When other girls walked after school to Selig's Drugstore for a soda, Jessie walked home alone. She declined invitations to sleigh rides and harvest moon picnics on glorious Flint Hills and to summer boating and swimming parties on the Walnut. Thus it was a shock to the Kooglers when Jessie began walking home from school with a young man named Ray Tack. He was a likeable young man from a large and popu-

6

lar Roman Catholic family, a minority group in the predominately Protestant community. As soon as summer vacation began the Kooglers and Jessie and Mrs. Black and her daughter Grace went to Colorado for a holiday. In the fall her parents reluctantly permitted Jessie to enter the University of Kansas at Lawrence as a special student in the Fine Arts School. The separation was an agony for her parents but they were consoled by the knowledge that Ray Tack would not be among the El Dorado boys and girls to enroll in the University.

During her two years at Lawrence, 1900 through 1902, Jessie studied drawing, composition, elocution, and physical training. She was graded I in all courses except drawing in which she made Grade II. In college a latent personality began to blossom. She became more confident than shy, more poised than awkward, more self-reliant than dependent on her parents. Even more important, she made friends.

Her roommate was a music student, Esther Louise Thayer of Wichita, Kansas, the granddaughter of General Sylvanus Thayer, known as the father of the U. S. Military Academy. The association marked the beginning of a lifelong friendship. Miss Thayer married J. W. Kirkpatrick, an El Dorado jeweler, whom Jessie regarded as a beloved brother. At a later period in her life she relied on him for advice and depended on him to look after her complicated business interests in El Dorado.

At Lawrence Jessie became better acquainted with four other El Dorado girls who were also art students. They were Flora and Cecil Leland and Tessie and Pearl Miller. During vacations Jessie and Flora Leland went on sketching trips through the El Dorado countryside and along the Walnut, their pockets stuffed with graham crackers against sudden hunger. Art was becoming a compulsive and consuming interest to Jessie.

At the end of the second year at Lawrence Jessie determined to continue her studies at the Art Institute of Chicago. But Dr. Koogler would not deviate from his firm opinion that while a lady could be pampered in a wish to learn to play the violin or the piano, no proper young lady of that day should be encouraged to study art unless it was painting flowers on china. Jessie saw the futility of trying her usual trick of getting her way—going to bed and refusing to budge until her parents gave in to her wishes—for this time they might let her remain forever between the covers. But there were other means to an end, and her renewed interest in young Ray Tack brought immediate results. Her interest in Tack was genuine and thus it was to continue until the day she died, when his gift of an abundance of red roses on the table by her bed was her final glimpse of earthly beauty. Dr. Koogler retreated and at length gave his consent for her enrollment at the Institute. This unprecedented revolt was her first step toward her ultimate destiny.

The Kooglers' concern for their inexperienced daughter alone in a big city was somewhat lessened when they learned that Dr. Miller was sending his two daughters to the Art Institute and that Flora Leland was also continuing her studies there. Jessie's roommate in Chicago was Pearl Miller, who later taught art in El Dorado.

When Jessie enrolled in the fall of 1902 she dropped the name Jessie and used her father's name and initial. She explained that the name Jessie had become odious to her because of its association with El Dorado's most notorious murderess, Jessie Morrison, whose shocking deed of cutting her rival's throat with a razor remains after sixty-five years the town's greatest scandal. Old friends, however, never became accustomed to the name change and continued to call her Jessie.

Nineteen-year-old Marion was enchanted with Chicago and the opportunities it offered for new and constant excitements. At last she could see a great number of original paintings and, more, she was privileged to meet and to talk to artists who painted some of them. At the Institute her associates were established academic artists of that day as well as young and unknown art students, some of whom were destined to change the course of American art. Marion spent many hours discussing art with her new friends and many more hours silently absorbing their theories of colors and techniques and listening to their debates on the merits of the so-called Modernists. She was definitely on the side of the Modernists.

With Pearl Miller she explored the city in an eagerness to know every facet of its cultural and entertainment life. Her characteristic impatience at delays probably saved her life the cold night of December 30, 1903, when she and Pearl, weary from standing in line for tickets at the new Iroquois Theatre where Eddie Foy was playing in *Mr. Bluebird,* decided to attend a less popular show. But one thousand, seven hundred and forty other persons bought tickets the night the Iroquois burned and six hundred and two of them were killed in the panic and fire.

In Chicago Marion Koogler came alive. The plain little girl from Kansas was suddenly as strikingly handsome as an Aztec princess. And indeed she looked like one with an abundance of straight black hair pulled tightly from a high forehead and braided into a knot which rested at the back of a long slender neck. Intense brown eyes reflected her mood and humor and observant friends judged her state of mind by the degree of their sparkle. Her strong classical features and regal bearing gave an impression of height although she was only slightly over five feet tall.

Marion Koogler's beauty is remembered by at least two other Art Institute students of that day. One is Olin Herman Travis, a well-known Texas artist, who was at that time an art student from Dallas. Although five years younger than she, he was among her friends and admirers. More than half a century later he recalled:

"Marion was tall and more handsome than beautiful, with a vibrant and positive personality. She was most active in student affairs. I was a bit in awe of her. I was very poor and she was known to be rich. I had a few dates with her, the dates consisting of taking her to a few school dances. I believe we went to the Field Museum which at that time was in Jackson Park. Also we sneaked off and went to a vaudeville show or two.

"But I never saw Marion again or heard of her or from her from 1915 until 1943. This was when Mrs. Travis was playing in the San Antonio Symphony and I had a one-man show at the Witte Museum. Marion sent word to me that she would like to see me. I was given directions about how to get to her house. I knew nothing of her circumstances and was astonished when I arrived. The first thing Marion said was 'Where is that coal black hair?' I made no comment about how she had changed."

The other student was Emily Edwards, San Antonio artist and writer, whose memory of Marion Koogler was brought sharply into focus when she saw a portrait bust thought to have been made during the Art Institute days. Although Miss Edwards had known Marion Koogler since she first came to San Antonio and even before her marriage to Dr. Atkinson, it was not until shortly before her death that Miss Edwards saw the bust for the first time and immediately recognized it as the portrait of a student she had known many years before at the Chicago Art Institute. Miss Edwards said:

"I was fifteen years old when I first went to the Institute and I did not know Marion Koogler but I knew who she was. Everyone knew by sight the handsome, high-colored, stunning girl named Marion Koogler. She was the type we called, in those days, a high stepper.

"I was astonished when I came face to face with the bust and I immediately exclaimed: 'That's Marion Koogler!' Until that moment I had never connected the student Marion Koogler with the San Antonio Marion Koogler. I wanted to go back up the stairs and tell Marion about it. But I did not, and I never saw her again. She never knew how great an impression she had made on me when I was fifteen and how much, from afar, I had admired her beauty and personality."

After graduating Marion continued to study at the Institute and was reluctant to leave the congenial environment and return to El Dorado. She felt an obligation, however, to spend the long vacations there and back in her old environment Marion once more became the Kooglers' adored and compliant daughter.

The threat of Ray Tack had been removed when he married, but he was replaced by a number of young men to whom Marion was briefly engaged. Each time the engagement failed to withstand Dr. Koogler's disapproval.

Dr. Koogler retired in 1912 and returned to Ohio. He selected the town of Marion because Clara Koogler's brothers, Sam and Chris Lippincott, and other Lippincott relatives lived there. Clara's long separation from the Lippincotts had been a constant sorrow to her.

Marion continued to spend part of each year in Chicago. The Art Institute recommended her to Dr. John Benjamin Murphy, a noted Chicago surgeon, when he consulted the faculty on an artist to illustrate his famous operations. He was the inventor of the Murphy Button, a device for rapid and accurate intestinal anastomosis. Marion loved her work as a medical illustrator and was disheartened when Dr. Koogler, appalled at her employment, peremptorily summoned her home.

Home was an unpretentious little house on East Center Street in Marion, Ohio. Now that Dr. Koogler had no income from his medical practice he lived almost as frugally as when they first settled in El Dorado. Marion had one advantage over El Dorado —it was closer to Chicago.

In 1913 Marion Koogler attended the first exhibition of modern art in the United States. It was the famed Armory Show which had opened in New York and now, from March 24 to April 16, a part of it was on exhibition at the Art Institute of Chicago. She was not among those students, teachers, and former students of the Institute who burned the artists in effigy and denounced the degenerate painters of Paris. On the contrary, it was the most thrilling aesthetic experience of her life. Not only did it change the course of Marion's life but it influenced the painting theories of many American artists and redirected the buying habits of a few collectors.

Since each of the four hundred and fifty-three items received careful and thoughtful examination, Marion made repeated visits to the galleries. She had her first comprehensive view of the art of Cezanne, Picasso, Braque, Gauguin, Pissarro, Van Gogh, Degas, and Renoir, all of whom someday would hang on her own walls, as would the works of some of the American Independents in the exhibition, such as Marin, Prendergast, Henri, Sloan, and Weber.

If Marion Koogler was bewildered, it was not due to the flat surfaces, the liberated and glowing colors and forms, or the controlled spaces of the canvases, but rather it was due to the furor the paintings created among some critics and spectators. Although her own paintings of that period faithfully followed the objective realism taught at the Institute, Marion's mind had not been equally disciplined.

Her fresh eyes saw nothing in Matisse's *La Femme Bleu* to inspire the hysterical effigy burning of the artist nor to give cause for Critic H. Effa Webster's alarmed cry that "our splendid Art Institute is being desecrated." She felt a sickening shock when she read that a local editor considered the "crazy quilt art . . . not fit for children's eyes . . . nasty, lewd, immoral, obscene, and scandalous."

After her last visit to the galleries Marion, in a golden glow of discovery, was on her way to take a train back home. Little Corah Mooney of El Dorado was a block away wishing she had Marion's Chicago address. Corah never forgot her astonishment when the two friends met face to face on a Chicago sidewalk. If Marion mentioned her rapturous art experience, Corah has no remembrance of it. Soon Marion rushed off, a wicker basket containing her favorite cat swinging on her arm, the colors of the canvases still vivid in her mind.

Marion made another attempt at a career in 1914 when she accepted an offer from the Marion Public Schools as substitute art supervisor. At the end of the year she had decided to make teaching her career and with a letter of recommendation set out to find a permanent place. The letter, dated June 21, 1915, was written by Henry A. Hartman, Superintendent of the Marion City Schools:

"To Whom It May Concern:

"This certifies that Miss Marion Koogler has been Supervisor of Art in the Marion Public Schools for one year supplying the regular Supervisor's place, during a leave of absence, and her work was eminently satisfactory.

"Miss Koogler is one of the best qualified art teachers I have ever known, and besides she is a skillful teacher. She teaches Art in a manner that arouses and develops the child's observation and enlarges his aesthetic nature.

"I unhesitatingly recommend Miss Koogler as the best and know that no one would make a mistake in employing her."

But again fatherly persuasion kept her at home. Besides, activities in El Dorado, Kansas, were altering the placid course of the Koogler way of life in Marion.

El Dorado's first successful oil well was brought in during September, 1915, and the town was soon in a boom. The surrounding grazing land was dotted with oil wells and the bluestem grass which from time beyond man's memory had withstood tornadoes, drouths, plagues of grasshoppers, and greedy Texas cows, died wherever oil hit it. Irate cattlemen stood guard over their pastures protecting the grass from the ravages of drilling equipment for they well knew that all their new wealth could never replace the grass God had given them.

Much of the Koogler acreage was under oil and gas leases. The lease money and prospects of wealth made little outward change in the Koogler household. The family continued to live in the little Center Street house, Clara Koogler went about her household chores with only a girl Lina in once a week to do the family laundry, and Marion continued to give private painting lessons.

In March, 1916, Marion Koogler was in New York to attend another memorable art show. It was the Forum Exhibition of Modern American Painters at the Anderson Galleries, the first showing of a comprehensive selection of modern American art. As on the occasion of the Armory Show the works of the vanguard of modern art exhibited at the Forum made a deep impression on her and influenced her later collection. Her catalogue of the exhibition, Number 159, is in the present McNay Library.

That same year Marion Koogler met a shy and modest young man named Don Denton McNay, who was manager of the Columbus, Delaware, and Marion Railway Company of Marion, Ohio. Their friendship perplexed her family and friends. Don McNay was ten years younger than Marion, but he was a hard-working, serious-minded young man.

Perhaps Dr. Koogler recalled his reason many years before for buying Marion a pony. At any rate, even he had to face the fact that his daughter was thirty-four years old and by now should have been a married woman with a family of her own. Dr. Koogler admitted that the boy was sober, industrious, and obviously very much in love.

But meanwhile, he suggested to Marion, why not take a holiday—perhaps she would like to visit old friends in El Dorado and spend Christmas in Chicago?

She did, and in December, 1916, Marion ended her winter holiday in Chicago at the home of a friend, Harriet Hurst. Two letters received from Don McNay while she was there were among her few personal papers when she died. He wrote of the difficulty in keeping the street cars operating in the heavy snow, gave news of the opening of a new track on David Street, reported a collision of one of the cars with her uncle's automobile, and added a few personal remarks:

"If your friends or your business conditions necessitate your staying until after Xmas, I'll not become peeved, even though I am anxious for you to return. Your good judgment should govern your deeds. . . . When you speak in your letters of those parties and all that 'butterfly stuff' I wonder what in the world you will do with a man of the other set, a social impossibility, who has no use for anyone but those he likes and would rather work a month than spend an hour at a reception. Marion, it would be utterly impossible for me to visit any one for more than a day or so, there's a little voice within me that always seems to say, 'maybe you're putting some one to some bother, maybe you are in the way.' Mother tells me almost every day I am getting queer and darn it all I try hard to be human and like other people but it seems that I just can't do it. . . . I am thankful for having that sort of a girl that Dad married and still having the one he got too. To me my mother is the most wonderful mother in all the world, it seems that all she lives for is her 'boys' and to see them do a wrong would break her heart. Every day she seems to grow dearer to me. . . . Marion, as you know, I ain't much of a fellow to put my feelings into words, but in my silent sort of

way, I want you to know that I am awful glad that you will be home in less than a week, time never went so slow as the past few weeks have. . . . I see by the time-table that the Chicago train is due at Marion at 6:10 p.m., suppose that this will be your train. I will be down and do the heavy work, help you home, you will be worn out and then after a visit with parents you will be ready to rest and then the next night you can invite the Irish out, if you are not too worn out. . . . This is about all I can think of to write, will tell you the rest of the news when I see you. My regards to Miss Hurst, tell her there are worse places than our town pump to drink at and that I would like to meet her face to face."

Don, the first of two sons of Samuel A. and Addie May Brewer McNay, was born in Chesterville, Ohio. He lived with his parents and younger brother, Fleet, at 123 East Farming Street in Marion. Don's personality combined characteristic traits Marion always responded to in others—a youthful sincerity, parental devotion, indifference to society, and a guileless honesty in personal relationships. Many years later, Marion Koogler told the mother of her first youthful sweetheart that she was from the beginning attracted to Don McNay because he was so much like Ray Tack.

The year 1917 not only brought drastic changes in the history of man but marked the end of Marion Koogler's own placid, little-girl dream world. A month after the United States went to war against Germany, the El Dorado, Kansas, oil field was extended southward when the Page-Lewis Oil Company brought in Koogler No. 1 on Dr. Koogler's Butler County land.

The certainty of wealth caused Dr. Koogler more concern than joy; thrift by now was a habit. His mind was further troubled by Marion's announced intention of marrying the McNay boy. Under pressure, he gave perfunctory consent.

Don had enlisted in the Army and was a sergeant in the Student Company No. 8, Quartermaster Corps, and under orders to report to Fort McIntosh in Laredo, Texas. There was no time for the big wedding for which Clara Koogler wept and on which Dr. Koogler frowned.

Marion Koogler and Don McNay were married in a simple ceremony on December 9, 1917, by Dr. Linius Strock of the Presbyterian Church. Dr. Koogler was a reluctant witness.

Both the bride and groom gave their ages as twenty-eight on the marriage license. Actually, Marion was a month and seven days under thirty-five and Don was twenty-four.

As a wedding present, Dr. Koogler gave his daughter one hundred and sixty acres of his Kansas land. She would need some security, he reasoned, since young Don manfully insisted that his bride would have to do the best she could on his meager army pay.

There was time for a brief honeymoon in Columbus, Ohio, where the couple posed for photographs in front of artificial palm trees.

Honeymoon photographs, Marion Koogler and Sgt. Don Denton McNay, Columbus, Ohio, 1917

Marion wore her wedding suit of gray plush, trimmed in gray fur and with a matching muff. Before leaving for Laredo she sent one of them to her parents and noted on the back of it:

> "We had these taken yesterday, the kind 'finished while you wait.' They were so poor of Don he wanted to destroy them but I persuaded him to let me send one to Dad and one to Mother McNay but you are not to show them to any one."

Laredo in 1918 retained the semblance of a raw border town and it was unprepared to meet the housing demands of wartime.

Honeymoon abode cottage in Laredo, Texas, where the McNays lived in 1918

After a long search the McNays found a place to begin housekeeping. The house was a low and crumbling adobe fronted by an open porch, shaded from the merciless sun by a scant and thirsty vine. A few trees struggled for sustenance in the wind-swept yard, bare of even a blade of grass. A patched, falling-down picket fence separated the little yard from the street which was thick with white dust. On the porch a lonely bird noisily protested its confinement in a dangling cage which moved slightly in the hot breeze.

Marion searched the shops for food supplies, cooked three meals a day in a kitchen that was as hot as the inside of the oven, and sweltered in the unaccustomed Texas heat. Only the absence of letters from her father marred her happiness. Clara Koogler wrote daily. In a letter dated April 14,

1918, she described what was probably a typical Sunday in the Koogler household in Marion.

"Dear Children:

"This is Sunday evening and the end of a well nigh perfect day. Much more like spring than any we have been having. Daddy went to church this morning. I did not go but had dinner ready when he got home. And if I do say it was a pretty fair dinner. Daddy brought ice cream which helped out a great deal. We both wished Don and Marion were here. Just after dinner Mrs. Dana called up and asked us to go riding, and what a ride we did have. . . . Then home and supper and now Daddy is asleep on the couch and I am a little tired and think we will both sleep well tonight. Must

13

not forget to tell you we saw several patches of snow along the way in sheltered places. The country is looking fine. The wheat is showing up some and saw so much plowed ground. Looks like the farmers are preparing to do their bit. Tomorrow we are expecting the plasterers to fix the pantry and Lina is due to come and wash. So you see it means another full day. Dr. Strock is expected home on furlough this week, will officiate at two weddings and expects to fill his pulpit next Sunday. Well, we would love to see you tonight and we are hoping and praying that you are both well and happy and may be restored to us again."

The next morning Mrs. Koogler added a few lines:

"Your fine letter of Wednesday came and so glad—and O the pictures! They are fine—and our Don and Marion are *all O.K.* Mother Mc just called up, told her we had letter, she is coming up soon, maybe this afternoon. This is a fine morning and all are well and hope our dear ones are also. Hope you have mail by this time. Think I missed writing a card just one day. How we will enjoy looking at all the pictures and studying them when we have time. Daddy joins in bushels of love."

Despite the heat and inconveniences the months spent in Laredo with Don McNay were the happiest ones of Marion Koogler's life and she cherished the memory of them through the years. There were not to be many of them, such as the one she described on a picture postcard she addressed to her father on June 19, 1918:

"Dear Folks: Been pretty hot today and am sweating like a 'hoss' but both are well and happy. Don been awfully busy today and I have not been idle. Jane washed today. Rec. your card of Sat. and papers noticed Daddy directed the ones we got yesterday. No news only that it is pretty hot and we are both

equal to three squares a day and just finished some Loganberry 'glass eye' as a night cap. Hope this finds all well at home. Bushels of love from Your Children."

Shortly Don McNay was ordered to Camp Joseph E. Johnston in Jacksonville, Florida, and because of army restrictions Marion could not go with him. They traveled together as far as San Antonio and stayed at the old Menger Hotel on Alamo Plaza until Don's departure. His company assembled at the Alamo for the march to the railroad station and it was before this historic monument to freedom that they told each other goodbye.

Thereafter, to Marion the Alamo became a personal symbol and the memory of that day would bring her back to it and later influence her $15,000 bequest for a San Antonio chapel provided it follow the exterior design of the old shrine.

Marion returned to her parents' home in Ohio, hoping to be able soon to join her young husband in Florida. The reunion came much earlier than she expected but under tragic circumstances she had not foreseen. A few weeks after their parting, news of Don McNay's serious illness reached her while she was attending a Sunday night movie with a young cousin, Jessie Lippincott. The first train out of town was due to leave in less than an hour but Marion suddenly realized she had no money for a ticket and there was not enough time to wait for her parents to return from church. But the resourceful young Jessie worked for a loan company and using her key to enter the office took enough from the till for train fare to Jacksonville. Jessie Lippincott (Winkworth) referred to this incident as the time she robbed a bank for Marion. In the years ahead her grateful cousin found many opportunities to repay Jessie for her daring deed.

Don McNay died on October 25, 1918, ten months after his marriage, and his body was returned to Marion for a military

14

funeral and burial in the Koogler family plot.

The sorrow of the tragic end of her marriage to Don McNay never healed and Marion Koogler's later empty and futile pursuit of personal happiness resulted in four marriages each ending in divorce.

Marion remained with her parents in their new home, the old P. O. Sharpless house at 334 East Center Street, a stately, two-story, century-old brick house. The lovely home brought her little pleasure for her thoughts were only of a hot little adobe house in Laredo. Again she resorted to the childhood habit of taking to her bed, as good a place as any to mark time when nothing in life appeared worth the bother of getting out of it. Happiness then and always was an empty bird cage slowly swinging in a hot and dusty breeze from the Rio Grande.

Even the excitement of the constantly increasing oil wells on the Koogler Butler County land failed to rouse Marion from her state of depression.

As the years passed, the oil boom in El Dorado became a permanent condition. Jessie Perry Stratford, an El Dorado newspaper executive, made a shrewd estimate of the Koogler oil wells in 1935:

"These Koogler leases have a unique history. From the time of the initial well to the present, the Koogler property has proved a steady producer. It has character, stamped by dependability. None of the 20,000 barrels-for-one-day about it. But rather, a steady, day-after-day, year-after-year production. According to figures given out by the Empire Company, 104 wells have been drilled on this property and over four million barrels of oil have been produced. The company has faith that it will be producing in 1950."

And indeed it was, and even surpassed the hopeful 1935 prediction. At present (1967) some of the wells are in the secondary recovery stage and it is thought possible that new drilling methods will extend wells deeper into untapped oil flows.

But to Dr. Koogler the oil wealth brought only increasing problems and confusion to his last years which he had fully expected to pass in tranquillity. He invested his income in stocks, bonds, real estate, and other securities and carefully budgeted his living expenses from dividends. He employed his attorney friend William P. Moloney of Marion to take over the multiplicity of legal details involving leases, titles, taxes, and other matters and tried not to worry about his unaccustomed and overwhelming responsibilities. But Dr. Koogler worried more about Marion than he had at any other time in her life. He knew his years, if not his days, were few and his greatest wish for her was marriage to a substantial and mature man who would guard both her personal welfare and her personal wealth.

He deliberately set out to find a man possessing the qualifications he considered essential in his Marion's husband. Dr. Koogler found his man. He was Charles Newton Phillips, a prominent banker of Marion.

Phillips, older than Marion, had an established and sound position in the business life of the town and his personal financial condition was known to be secure. Moreover, as a bachelor he was socially popular and his agreeable appearance, charming manners, and reputation as a witty and interesting conversationalist made him an exceedingly eligible one. Dr. Koogler was further pleased that Phillips was a deacon in the Presbyterian Church.

Marion Koogler McNay married the man of her father's choice on January 12, 1921. Everyone agreed that it was a perfect match and the Kooglers were ecstatic in their happiness and relief.

The Phillipses moved in with the Kooglers and Marion pursued her new role with grim determination. In the past she had selected clothes with an indifferent eye but now she shopped in New York at the most exclusive shops whose exotic creations soon established the new Mrs. Phillips as

15

one of Marion's best-dressed women. She entertained extensively in her parents' home, vacationed at the accepted fashionable resorts, and, in general, appeared to conform to the town's idea of the proper young society matron.

Marion's entree into the inner circle of Marion society was through her sister-in-law Carrie, wife of James Phillips, whose splendid home was the scene of the town's most lavish entertainment. Charles's other brother, Frank, was married to Marion's close friend, Alta.

Although Marion knew from the beginning that the marriage was a tragic error and could not possibly succeed, she hid her unhappiness from her elated father. If the marriage added nothing to her personal felicity, it intensified her will and determination and erased the lingering traces of shyness.

Marion Koogler McNay Phillips was a dramatically exciting woman, high-spirited and daring. Her entrance into a room, it was said, was as effective and memorable as that of the late Mrs. Marie Antoinette Murdock, the elocution teacher of the distant days in El Dorado. There was little time in which to pursue her favorite hobbies of painting and writing poetry and only on rare occasions did she resort to either as a means of self-expression. But one such occasion was the death of President Warren G. Harding whom she greatly admired despite the wreck he had made of the marriage of the James Phillipses. She expressed her sorrow in a poem which was published in the *Times* of El Dorado and which she carefully clipped and kept among her personal papers and mementoes.

Dr. Koogler died in 1924 and was buried next to Don Denton McNay in the Koogler plot. His death brought an end to the Phillips' marriage. Dr. Koogler's and Marion's good friend Mr. Moloney was entrusted with the divorce proceedings and Clara and Marion went to live in St. Petersburg, Florida.

The Phillips' divorce was granted on May 25, 1925, and in an out-of-court settlement Phillips received $150,000 and waived claim on Marion Koogler's considerable personal property.

Many years after Dr. Koogler's death, his daughter made a frank revelation of circumstances of her marriage to Phillips. Marion showed no indication or even a trace of bitterness or reproach toward her father for his selection of Phillips as the ideal husband. Her dear father, she told her friend, could not be held responsible for an error in judgment.

Marion and Mrs. Koogler returned to Marion to be present at a ceremony in February, 1926, in the First Presbyterian Church dedicating a fine pipe organ they had given in memory of Dr. Koogler and Don McNay. The town of Marion had never meant as much to Marion Koogler as had El Dorado and now it became a lonely place of painful memories. Again life was without purpose and Clara worried when Marion took to her bed for a prolonged stay. When Marion suggested making a sentimental journey to San Antonio Clara readily agreed.

From her window in the Menger Hotel, Marion could look down upon the Alamo where she and Don had parted seven years before. In a way, it was like coming home.

The old-world atmosphere of San Antonio inspired Marion to take up painting again and in her new surroundings her melancholia disappeared. She made new friends: the witty and charming Florence Jacoby and her beautiful daughter Mimi; Mary Aubrey Keating, the talented artist wife of Dr. Peter Keating; Anita Arneson, a gifted leader in the city's music and literary activities; and Dr. Donald Taylor Atkinson, a prominent ophthalmologist.

Not only was Dr. Atkinson interested in the general field of art but he was himself an amateur painter although in a decidedly primitive style. When he learned of Marion's experience as an illustrator for the famous Dr. Murphy, he asked her to make drawings of some of his operations.

Dr. Atkinson was born in 1874 in New Brunswick, Canada. He settled in San Antonio in 1913 after extensive travels and experiences as a frontier doctor in different sections of the country. An inveterate traveler, he combined his wanderlust and his profession on expeditions to Mexico and to Haiti to research leprosy and yaws and to other remote areas in pursuit of other baffling diseases. He was the inventor of surgical instruments for eye operations, an authority on cancer of the throat, and had written a number of books on his varied specialties.

Clara and Marion found Dr. Atkinson interesting and delightful company and both agreed that he reminded them of the late Dr. Koogler. Like Dr. Koogler, Dr. Atkinson was a staunch Presbyterian. When he asked Marion to marry him, both Marion and Clara thought the marriage would have pleased Dr. Koogler.

Guests at the house-finishing party for construction workers were entertained by Spanish dancers in the patio

II. THE MIDDLE SPAN

It did not seem an anomaly the night of the long-remembered housewarming at the Atkinson house that the exceedingly few paintings on the walls were ones Marion Koogler had painted in her early student days.

But in view of her subsequent consuming interest in collecting, the void is almost incredible. Only a few days before, a hopeful local artist had tried to sell Marion a cactus painting and she had observed, as though she had just discovered the fact and was herself surprised, that there was no suitable space on the walls to hang paintings. The numerous windows and glass doors framed the outside landscapes of foliage, flowers, fountains, and the intensely blue Texas skies. These were the only pictures she had in mind when the house was planned.

Unlike Mrs. Potter Palmer who built a Chicago castle with walls high enough to hang paintings three deep, Marion Koogler did not plan wall height nor space for the display of paintings. Marion Koogler's only concern at the time was that the walls be sufficiently thick and that their texture suggest the old Spanish palm finish. Wall space was greatly reduced by her insistence on numerous wide windows and doorways which would assure a maximum of circulating fresh air and exposure to morning and afternoon sunlight.

Marion Koogler's house was her creative masterpiece, a perfection she could never achieve in her painting. The planning, building, and furnishing of the Sunset Hills mansion was to her an exciting and highly satisfactory aesthetic adventure from the beginning to its completion. Dr. Atkinson chafed over the delayed European trip but his wife refused to agree to his frequent suggestions that they go away while the house was under construction. Until an illness forced her into a hospital, Marion Koogler was constantly on the job. While she was in the hospital the entire outside of the house was finished in smooth plaster and painted, and when she came home she ordered it retextured in a rough finish and repainted.

Her penchant for peacocks influenced both interior and exterior accents. She selected a stylized peacock motif for the stencil pattern for the over-all dining room ceiling. A rug of deepest blue background, patterned with the proud bird which symbolizes immortality, was made in China from her design. The theme is repeated in large Talavera tile friezes, made from her sketches by master craftsmen in Puebla, Mexico, which dominate the exterior walls of the patio. The rose window of San Antonio's Mission San Jose inspired the central pool in the elongated octagonal patio.

In the course of working out the intricate arrangement of brick walls in the inner courtyard, Marion Koogler became a proficient brick-layer. With the assistance of Tony Lozano, a San Antonio tile maker, she designed and installed the smaller tiles on bases of fountains and planters and on stair risers. Many of the *cancelas* and graceful iron grilles were of her design, executed by local foundries.

The furnishings and decorations of the house and gardens were not limited to Spanish colonial but reflected a variety of periods

Aerial view of Sunset Hills, 1929

and trends. Marion Koogler sought out old wrought iron lamps and *torcheres,* wall brackets, antique chandeliers, and unusual hardware for inclusion in the permanent features of the house. From New Orleans came old grilles and a plantation slave bell. The carved front of an old Spanish chest and two caryatids, items she had long cherished, were set in the wall beneath a grille in one of the hallways.

Native plants and trees, tall pines and palmettos, rare cycades and palms from Hawaii, magueys and yuccas from Mexico, and a variety of large exotic cacti soon covered the once dusty caliche hill. Twenty-three boxcars of mammoth red granite boulders from Texas' Marble Falls area, a birthday present, were dumped around the periphery. Gradually the surrounding acreage was turned into gardens, shaded walks, terraces, and pavilions, and the landscape assumed its proper relation to the house.

The house at Sunset Hills was opened to thousands of San Antonians at two memo-

Side entrance to Sunset Hills and, below, garden detail

rable housewarming receptions in 1929. The first was a house-finishing celebration for construction workers and their families and friends. The festivities were repeated the following night for members of the medical profession, various cultural organizations and civic groups, and for personal friends.

Kansas bullfrogs which had arrived from El Dorado in time for the parties croaked happily from the patio pool in competition with the orchestra on the patio balcony and with the harpist in the main hall. A group of Spanish dancers and musicians performed in the central court.

The event also served to introduce Marion Koogler to San Antonio. Some who attended the receptions remember their

Top—Approach to dining room entrance from garden

Bottom—Detail of central patio

Top—Early view of patio showing peacock tile mural

Bottom—Early view of first floor library

Top—Main entrance to reception hall showing stenciled archways

Bottom—Detail of entrance hall and stenciled wall beams

Patio viewed from upstairs loggia and, below, peacock dining room (early views)

hostess as a slender, vivacious woman, beautifully gowned, and wearing Russian garnets. Shortly after the house was opened Dr. and Mrs. Atkinson made their long-delayed trip to Europe.

The first oil painting purchased by Marion Koogler was Diego Rivera's *Delfina Flores* which for more than twenty-five years remained almost unknown but which today is one of the Mexican artist's most popular portraits. The painting was first shown in 1927, the year in which it was painted, at the Witte Museum in San Antonio at Diego Rivera's unrecorded first exhibition in the United States. This was sponsored by the San Antonio Art League and arranged by one of its members, Miss Emily Edwards, who was studying in Mexico with Rivera at that time. The exhibit is memorable in San Antonio art circles because it ignited a city-wide controversy when the artist's offer to paint the backdrop in the new auditorium for a mere $500 was indignantly rejected by the city.

Delfina Flores was purchased from the show by Mrs. Roy Beitel of San Antonio who later sold it to Mrs. McNay. The charming portrait of a wistful little Mexican girl would have found a congenial background at Sunset Hills where it is presently hanging but it was left on loan so long at the Witte Museum that the Art League regarded it as another gift from Mrs. McNay.

Although it might be said that the present McNay Collection began with the purchase of *Delfina*, it was not until 1931 that the collection was activated.

That year Marion Koogler attended the Eleventh International Exhibition of Water Colors, Pastels, Drawings, Monotypes, and Miniatures at the Art Institute of Chicago and purchased fourteen watercolors, the favorite medium for her own painting and one in which she had been trained. Nine of her purchases remain in the Museum, the nucleus of what was in time to grow into an impressive collection of American and European watercolors.

Penciled notes on the page margins of the 1931 catalogue, presently in the McNay Library, indicate Mrs. McNay's interest in items she did *not* buy, such as No. 26, Paul Cezanne's *Still Life*. She drew a sketch of it and noted: "Hanging next to Friesz nude. Red cloth, red chair, l. to r. fruit, b. glass, n. bottle, trees green, left background n. with red right background."

The nine watercolors which she took back to Sunset Hills and which are still there are, as they appeared in Marion's price catalogue:

No. 39. Raoul Dufy, *Flight of the Birds*, $375.

No. 43. E. Othon Friesz, *Nude with Algerian Draperies*, $160.

No. 170. Ethel Walker, *Portrait: Valerie*, $150.

No. 234. Emil Armin, *Canyon*, $100.

No. 242. Peggy Bacon, *The Painter*, $15. (drawing)

No. 306. Walt Dehner, *Banana Bellies*, $100.

No. 326. Anne Goldwaite, *Outdoors*, $100.

No. 354. Joseph W. Jicha, *Late Afternoon Bahamas*, $300.

No. 382. Ward Lockwood, *Canyon, Gray Day*, $150.

Before leaving Chicago she made her first purchase from the Chester H. Johnson Gallery. It was a watercolor by George Grosz, whose work had been prominent in the German section of the Institute's annual exhibit. *Street Scene in Paris* remains in the Museum collection.

At Sunset Hills Marion Koogler took down her own watercolors and replaced them with her new purchases. She added a studio room over the garage and returned to painting, soon becoming prominent in local artist groups. Most of her friends were active in the Art League and the San Antonio Conservation Society to which she also belonged.

On occasions Marion accompanied Dr. Atkinson on his foreign travels; one she enjoyed greatly was a boat trip down the west coast of Mexico and Central America to Cartagena, Chile. The coastal villages offered a rich field for the doctor's interest in yaws and leprosy. While he sought out interesting cases in the jungles, Marion painted the bright tropical scenery of Mexico, the handsomely costumed Indians of Guatemala and Central America, and the old colonial towns of Chile. In general, however, she did not share her husband's thirst for travel and much of the time he globetrotted without her. In the meantime she discovered Taos, New Mexico, and spent part of every summer there accompanied by the compatible Georgia Maverick Harris who shared her interest in cacti, costumes, and colonial Spanish craftsmanship, or by Cousin Jessie Lippincott who had come from Marion, Ohio, to live at Sunset Hills.

In the agreeable and congenial atmosphere of the Taos art colony of the late 1920's and 1930's Marion found new friends and renewed old friendships with artists she had known in her student days in Chicago. Even in Taos where individuality was rampant and unrepressed, Marion Koogler was a stunningly flamboyant figure and in such a setting could indulge her fondness for colorful costumes and dramatic hats. Taos was as exciting and provocative to Marion in her forties as Chicago had been in her twenties.

She met the unique community's Bohemian personalities, some genuine and some even talented and articulate, at the home of Mabel Dodge Luhan who had been the social dictator of Taos since 1916. Visitors of importance or of special interest usually found their way to the hospitable Luhan house on the edge of the Pueblo of Taos which one of the visitors, D. H. Lawrence, called "that center of twittering malice."

At Mabel Luhan's Marion Koogler met Victor Higgins and his good friend Andrew Dasburg, two veteran Taos artists. Hig-

Marion Koogler McNay in Taos—in such a setting she could indulge her fondness for colorful costumes.

gins' studio was one of the guest houses on the Luhan estate. It is possible that Marion had known Higgins, one year younger than she, at the Art Institute where they studied at the same time. Despite his early residence in Taos, Higgins was regarded as a Chicago painter and had been a consistent exhibitor and award winner at the Institute since 1914. Watercolors by both Higgins and Dasburg entered Marion Koogler's rapidly growing collection.

Not only was she regarded as a liberal patron of Taos art, but two of her own watercolors were accepted in the 1931 Annual Exhibition of Painters and Sculptors of the Southwest at the Museum of New Mexico. They were *Arroyo Seco* and *Gateway, Taos.*

Marion Koogler was in Taos during the summers of 1929 and 1930 when John Marin painted the New Mexican landscape with unusual crispness. Eventually

27

she acquired three of his watercolors, including *Taos,* dated 1930.

From Kenneth Miller Adams, a native of Kansas and a former Chicago Art Institute student, she purchased a number of watercolors, crayons, and lithographs of New Mexican scenes. She particularly admired the Marin-like watercolors of John Ward Lockwood, another Kansan and one-time chairman of The University of Texas Art Department, and acquired four of his Taos scenes.

The absence of a Georgia O'Keeffe painting in the McNay Taos group can only lead to the speculation that perhaps the ladies did not like each other. At that period in Mrs. McNay's collecting, acquisition was largely influenced by friendship with the artist. Almost certainly they knew each other for they moved in the same circles when both were students at the Institute in 1904, and in 1908 and 1909 when Miss O'Keeffe worked in advertising art in Chicago.

Whatever the reason for the omission of an O'Keeffe, it is regrettable. Surely, placed on a purely aesthetic basis, O'Keeffe's interpretation of New Mexico was both spiritually and artistically in harmony with Marion Koogler's taste, particularly as exemplified in *Black Cross* and *Rancho Church.*

The friendship motive is evidenced by the presence of most of the Taos artists in the present Collection.

The Swedish-born Bror Julius Olsson Nordfeldt had early discovered the pictorial appeal of the art of the New Mexico santeros and this mutual interest alone would have been sufficient to establish a rapport with Marion Koogler. But he was also an old classmate from the Art Institute and later a teacher in Wichita, Kansas, and at The University of Texas. The two Nordfeldt pastels in the Collection are Kansas scenes, both inscribed.

In Taos, Marion renewed an acquaintance with Nordfeldt's friend and former student, Raymond Jonson, from whom she purchased *Rising Moon,* one of his Universe Series.

Although the brief exposure of Leon Kroll and Robert Henri to Taos predated her visits, Mrs. McNay eventually acquired nudes by each of them.

Other Taos acquisitions included watercolor paintings of Indians by Einor Lundquist and Joseph A. Imhof; lithographs by Herbert A. Dunton and Arnold Ronnebeck; etchings by Howard Cook, C. E. Strausenback, and Birger Sandzen of Lindsborg, Kansas; a drawing by Datus Myers, an old friend from Chicago days; woodblocks by Gustave Baumann, who studied with her at the Art Institute; watercolors by Cady Wells, William Sommer, Olive Rush, Emil Bisttram, Boardman Robinson, Millard Sheets, Russell Cowles; a pastel by Randall Davey; an oil by Maurice Sterne, and John Sloan's 1928 *Self Portrait* in oil, a gift of the artist.

A new vitality and approach to Marion Koogler's random collecting became apparent in 1933. That was the year she met Mrs. Edith Gregor Halpert, director of the Downtown Gallery in New York.

In the spring she saw an exhibit at the Museum of Modern Art called "American Sources of Modern Art," designed to show the influence of the ancient art of the Americas on American painters. One of the paintings, *Girl With Flowers,* a 1911 pastel by Max Weber, led her to Mrs. Halpert's gallery which handled Weber's work.

She not only purchased the Weber, but went away with some other gems: a Jules Pascin oil, *Two Girls in an Armchair,* and a watercolor, *Landscape With Animals;* George Overbury "Pop" Hart's oil, *Flower Woman* (no longer in the Collection), and a watercolor *Arab Bathing His Horse;* and William Zorach's watercolor, *Popham Beach,* on the back of which the artist wrote: "To Marion Atkinson, recording a very pleasant visit—New York—Nov. 8th, 1933."

Either because of Mrs. Halpert's gentle

prodding or because of more personal reasons, Pascin and Hart were well represented in Mrs. McNay's purchases. At one time she owned six Hart paintings and almost all of his graphic works including the award-winning lithograph, *Springtime New Orleans,* which is said to have immortalized a Vieux Carre hangout of the two blithe roisterers. Mrs. McNay's catalogue of a Hart exhibition at the Downtown Gallery contains a small pasted-in watercolor sketch by Hart and inscribed by Mrs. Halpert "With appreciation to a real pioneer." Mrs. McNay's Pascin holdings included a scrap book record of the artist's travels in southern United States and the Caribbean purchased from Mrs. Halpert in 1934.

Mrs. McNay found in Mrs. Halpert a kindred spirit in her appreciation and feeling for primitive art. Once, following a conversation on that subject, Marion Koogler remarked that she would send one of her Nubian goats to the distinguished art dealer. Mrs. Halpert, expecting a piece of African sculpture, became somewhat alarmed when she later learned the present was to be a live pedigreed goat from Sunset Hills.

Many years later, Mrs. Halpert reminisced about Marion Koogler: "As a collector she was intensely interested in what she was buying and made certain that the individual example was, in her opinion, the best of those offered to her. This type of buyer is not prevalent today, as the motivations in collecting now include 'being hip,' shock value for animated after-dinner conversation, and of course the investment angle. Them was the good old days! The Nubian goat story is an example of her true enthusiasm for what she obtained from a dealer. She was so delighted with her purchases that she wished to send me a rare gift. It was a beautiful gesture, but a little difficult to house such a gift, despite the fact that I had a backyard on 13th Street."

Marion Koogler was in Chicago in September, 1933, to see the monumental Century of Progress exhibition, which was in staggering contrast to the now almost forgotten World's Columbian Exposition of her childhood. But modern art was not without apologists and the presence of the work of Van Gogh prompted a debate over the issue of whether a canvas painted without inward or mental sensibility could be considered art. In other words, Van Gogh was mad and his work incomprehensible and only a few with as much courage as money owned his paintings. As an investment the artist was highly speculative and definitely risky.

But six of the thirteen Van Goghs in the Century of Progress Gallery 47, the one most frequently visited by Marion Koogler, were owned by private collectors and three were lent by dealers. She studied every brush stroke of the Institute's superb yellow *Bedroom at Arles* of which Art Critic C. J. Bulliet had written: "Yellow, the psychiatrist will tell you, in doses like that, is the very hue of madness." Number 387, a small (12½″ x 24″) oil on paper on canvas, *Women of the Fields,* painted in 1890 in Auvers, was lent by the Chester H. Johnson Gallery. A year later Mrs. McNay bought the little painting for $15,000 and thus became the first owner of a Van Gogh in Texas.

All the symptoms of a confirmed collector's incurable acquisitiveness became evident as a result of the Century of Progress exhibition. Marion Koogler met the problem of the lack of wall space in her house by adding new rooms and using the walls of hallways and stairways. Before she left Chicago in 1933 she stopped by Chester H. Johnson's Gallery and selected another group of ten watercolors. Six which remain in the present Collection are: Paul Signac, *Pontrieux;* Segonzac, *Fall Landscape;* Eugene Boudin, *Beach Scene;* Sir William Orpen, *Crucifix by the Wayside;* Pierre Bonnard, *Autumn Landscape;* Mary Cassatt, *Head of a Girl.*

Unfortunately the four that got away,

apparently in subsequent trades, were watercolors or washdrawings by Matisse, Gauguin, Chagall, and Cezanne.

Elsewhere in the United States, and on a larger scale, other pioneer collectors were exposing the public to modern art through bequests. Slowly modern art through familiarity was assuming a degree of respectability. The Los Angeles County Museum was the proud though somewhat bewildered possessor of the Mrs. and Mrs. William Preston Harrison Collection. The Art Institute of Chicago was the beneficiary of the foresight and taste of Mrs. Potter Palmer and the Metropolitan had acquired the Havemeyer Collection. The Lillie P. Bliss Collection was in the Museum of Modern Art. The fabulous collection of the Cone sisters was destined for the Baltimore Museum if, in accordance with Miss Claribel Cone's will, the city could prove it was ready for modern art.

Ready or not, San Antonio had the Marion Koogler Collection and Sunset Hills was always open to anyone who cared to see it. The double iron gateway to the estate was never closed and many strangers who wandered off the highway and into the grounds thinking they were in a public park were hospitably received and frequently invited inside the house.

Some of the collection had been exhibited in 1932 at the Witte Museum. The exhibition, arranged by Director Ellen Quillin and Curator Eleanor Onderdonk, included forty-eight watercolors and four of Marion Koogler's own New Mexican paintings. Two years later the collection had materially increased and included drawings and watercolors by Modigliani, Derain, Vlaminck, Picasso, Toulouse-Lautrec, Dufy, and Forain.

The depression accomplished what public resistance failed to do: It halted the advance of Modern Art. Marion Koogler's picture money, as she termed the budgeted expenditure for collecting, was modest when compared to funds available to other collectors but it was little affected by the economic disaster. She continued to make purchases and her collection benefited considerably by the collapse of the art market.

However, a costly divorce from Dr. Atkinson brought about a temporary cessation in new art purchases. Dr. Atkinson apparently failed to live up to Dr. Koogler's measurements. The ten-year marriage ended October 30, 1936. In an out-of-court settlement, Marion Koogler kept possession of her home and twenty-three acres of the hundred and thirty-two of the original Sunset Hills tract and retained her personal holdings and property. Her name before marriage was restored. Dr. Atkinson married Wanda Wiley, a Texas girl who had had a brief movie career in silent films, and continued his world travels. Shortly before his death in 1958 Dr. Atkinson published *Texas Surgeon, An Autobiography* which is a somewhat singular autobiography. Ten entire years of his life, those in which he was married to Marion Koogler, are missing from an otherwise full account of a life fully lived.

A chance meeting on a lonely road in the Sangre de Cristo Mountains in 1934 with Ruth and Dalzell Hatfield of the prominent Los Angeles art gallery was the real beginning of the present Marion Koogler McNay Collection.

The Hatfields and Gina Knee, an artist from Marietta, Ohio, stopped to offer aid to a stalled Cadillac. The occupants were Marion Koogler and Georgia Maverick Harris who had been sketching in the mountains. Mrs. McNay had known Miss Knee since 1930 and, in fact, had just bought *Indian Dance*, one of her watercolors, but the Hatfields were strangers to her. Mr. Hatfield soon had the automobile in order and before going their separate ways Mrs. McNay invited the Hatfields and Miss Knee for cocktails the next day.

Not only did the Hatfields change the pattern of Mrs. McNay's collecting but their life-long friendship immeasurably enriched her life. They filled a void of associates who shared her knowledge and

Dalzell Hatfield showing Chagall's *Dream Village* which
was added to Mrs. McNay's growing collection

appreciation of art. The Hatfields found
her as knowledgeable as any collector of
their wide acquaintance.

Dalzell Hatfield and his Texas-born wife
Ruth Massie founded the Dalzell Hatfield
Gallery in Los Angeles in 1925 and as art
pioneers in the area were largely responsible for the cultural boom in Los Angeles
by influencing private collections and spon-
soring California artists such as Millard
Sheets, Russell Cowles, Richard Haines,
and Dan Lutz. When Mr. Hatfield died
in 1963, Art Critic Arthur Millier said of
him that he set standards of quality that
"helped to educate the rather provincial
art taste of an area destined to become

a world metropolis" and he observed that
to the Hatfields art was not solely a business but a way of life. Marion Koogler
received a full share of the warmth, understanding, and interest which they had
for both artists and art patrons.

That fall Mrs. McNay and the Hatfields
were in New York to see the first comprehensive Van Gogh exhibition in the United
States when the artist again was the victim
of hackneyed journalistic attacks and his
madness and the ear-cutting episode retold
in detail.

The three visited the exhibition at the
Museum of Modern Art for seven successive days. The penciled descriptive notes

31

on page margins in Mrs. McNay's catalogue indicate her excited reaction to the artist's vibrant colors and brush strokes.

While in New York she bought two majestic masterpieces of French painting from the Hatfields — Henri Rousseau's *Landscape with Milkmaids* and Paul Gauguin's *Sister of Charity*. The two oil paintings had just arrived in the United States and came into Mr. Hatfield's possession in a most casual way. The owner, a Norwegian ship captain, had first taken them to a dealer in old masters who suggested Mr. Hatfield as the logical buyer for modern French art.

The Hatfields and Mrs. McNay had a luncheon engagement that day and while Mr. Hatfield negotiated with the Norwegian the ladies waited at the hotel. And when he finally returned luncheon was further delayed while the paintings were unwrapped for viewing. When at last the three sat down to a very late luncheon the occasion called for champagne. Marion Koogler had purchased the two superb paintings before leaving the Hatfields' hotel sitting room. It marked the beginning of the Hatfield-McNay dealer-client relationship which proved a formidable combination. Except for a few random or sentimental purchases, Mrs. McNay selected and purchased exclusively from the Hatfield Gallery from that time until her death in 1950.

At the present time the Rousseau and the Gauguin are valued at more than ten times their original price. For the charming 1906 Rousseau Mrs. McNay paid $6,500 and for the 1902 Tahitian Gauguin she paid $15,000.

Ruth Hatfield recalled: "When Marion purchased these two paintings it was the first time that she considered herself a real collector. Before that she bought what she happened to like or to help out artists. Of course this does not apply to the little Van Gogh, or to the Renoir and the Picasso watercolor which she bought, I believe, just a year before we met her and at very low depression prices. But when Marion purchased the Rousseau and the Gauguin, she already had vast knowledge of modern French and other nineteenth and twentieth century art. I can certainly say that no Texas collector started off with a greater knowledge of art or a more complete understanding of the living artists' problems than did Marion Koogler McNay."

On their return from annual buying trips to pre-war Europe, the Hatfields invariably stopped in San Antonio to show Mrs. McNay their new discoveries and acquisitions. On such a visit in 1937 they learned that Mrs. McNay was ill and that her hospital room was closed to visitors. They were preparing to leave for California when Marion Koogler telephoned and demanded to know why they were leaving without seeing her and she insisted that they bring their paintings immediately to her hospital room. When the Hatfields hesitated to break doctor's orders she snapped: "I'll tell that doctor whom I can see."

So the crates and portfolios of paintings were taken to the Santa Rosa Hospital and unpacked in a room where a 100-degree temperature was maintained for the benefit of the patient but to the extreme discomfort of the visitors. In this Turkish bath atmosphere Mr. Hatfield unpacked his new purchases and one by one propped them at the foot of the bed for Marion Koogler's consideration. She seemed unaware that both the Hatfields were faint from the oppressive heat.

At length she selected two of the paintings—El Greco's *Head of Christ,* price $30,000, and Winslow Homer's watercolor *Scotch Mist,* $10,000.

After her divorce from Dr. Atkinson, Marion Koogler's vacations in Taos became extended stays. In addition to artists, art patrons, and upper-level Bohemians, she had many friends among the Pueblo Indians. Her friendship with the Indians was more than a summer-time tourist acquaintanceship but one built on mutual understanding and responsiveness. She found in the Pueblo Indians the same fundamental characteristics that she later admired in the nuns of the Missionary Servants in San Antonio, an otherwise totally dissimilar group. With both groups Marion Koogler enjoyed a pleasant and happy association which was a part of her inward and secret existence and quite apart from her public life. She cherished these friendships and guarded them against outside encroachment as though the magic would disappear if exposed to public gaze.

The person most familiar with Marion Koogler's spiritual kinship with these two groups was her attorney, William P. Moloney of Marion, Ohio.

"It would require a document of considerable size to detail the many incidents that reflect the intimacy of the relationship between Mrs. McNay and the Pueblo Indians of New Mexico during the fifteen or more years she spent her summers among them," Mr. Moloney said.

"Her interest in the American Indian, particularly the Pueblo Indian, manifested itself in the latter part of 1920 and through 1930 when, health permitting, she spent her summers in New Mexico, in and around Santa Fe and Taos from where she visited all the pueblos from Taos on the north to Isleta south of Albuquerque.

"Indian art, culture, and ceremonials had a definite fascination for her since they represented the development of the ages of a people whom she admired exceedingly. She recognized in the Pueblo Indian a person of deep-rooted conviction who believed in the customs and traditions of his people. She looked upon their tribal dances and ceremonials as an exemplification of their faith and she often spoke of the Pueblo Indian as one who believed implicitly in a supreme being.

"It is easy to understand the friendship of Mrs. McNay for the Pueblo Indian. If there was one thing she disliked intensely it was 'veneer.' There is no trace of sham

or guile in the American Indian and this attracted her and resulted in a mutual friendship that did not find expression in words alone but in more tangible evidence of its existence.

"In the years that she was more or less in direct contact with the Pueblo Indian there were many evidences of this friendship but these were overshadowed by a manifestation of its existence in 1943.

"In that year there was introduced in Congress a bill known as HR 323 which provided for the exploration of Pueblo land in New Mexico preliminary to the construction of dams in the middle Rio Grande. That measure, if pursued to its ultimate conclusion, would have destroyed at least two pueblos—San Ildefonso and San Felipe—and damaged several others, to say nothing of the shrines and sacred places of the Pueblos along the middle Rio Grande.

"As soon as this matter came to Mrs. McNay's attention she requested the San Antonio Conservation Society to file a formal protest and she directed that no expense be spared and nothing be left undone to prevent this disaster.

"A public hearing was held on this bill by the committee on Indian affairs of the House of Representatives on May 25 and 26, 1943, and thereafter extensive and almost continuous protests were filed with the committee. Finally after many moons and after much talk and effort, the bill was defeated in committee and the Pueblos and their shrines and sacred places spared.

"Mrs. McNay received many expressions of gratitude for her active assistance in this matter but the gratitude of the Pueblo Indians was best expressed by the ninety-two-year-old Governor of Santo Domingo when he simply said 'That lady, my friend, God bless him.'"

The Marion Koogler McNay Art Institute's collection of colonial Spanish and Indian arts and crafts is the fortunate result of the founder's interest in the natives of the Southwest and her appreciation and feeling for their art.

At the time Mrs. McNay was purchasing the work of the Taos colony of artists, she was also acquiring the work of Indian artists. Some of them were the first American Indians to emerge as recognized artists—Harrison Begay, Fred Kabotie, Tonita Peña, Julian Martínez, Abel Sánchez, and others. The ceramic of the famous María Martínez of San Ildefonso and other contemporary potters, the woodcarving of José Dolores López and of other descendants of colonial Spanish carvers, and the weaving and silver of contemporary Indian craftsmen were added to her collection.

A search for old *santos*—primitive religious images carved and painted on panels by the early colonists and their descendants—took Marion Koogler and Georgia Maverick Harris, her constant companion on such adventures, to old churches, chapels, and homes in remote mountain villages. The success of her search is best indicated by the McNay Collection of *bultos* and *retablos,* each a primitive though devout conception of an orthodox Christian saint. These treasures are presently and permanently displayed in a small gallery in the Marion Koogler McNay Art Institute which was designed after the charming chapels often found in the pueblos of New Mexico.

One of Marion Koogler's rare finds is a large carved crucifixion, considered unique in the field of New Mexican colonial art because the cross is represented by a carved and painted Spanish sword. Equally choice is an early and intact painting on an animal skin which portrays a charming and naive San Gabriel.

Mrs. McNay's annual purchases in the Southwest eventually became a vast accumulation of colonial New Mexican benches, cabinets, carts, chests, ornamental iron objects, and Chimayo blankets and rugs; Navajo weaving; old Hopi and Zuni kachinas; costumes, beads, silver, baskets, and pottery.

That Mrs. McNay was permitted to witness the secret and, at that time, outlawed flagellation rites of New Mexican Penitente Brotherhood indicates their confidence in her.

At times she joined in Indian tribal dances and on one such occasion a prominent San Antonio attorney watching a dance group in the plaza of Rancho de Taos was considerably startled when one of them stepped out of line and affectionately greeted him. He was even more astonished when he recognized the Indian as his sometime client, Marion Koogler.

She was always welcome in their pueblos and allowed freedom to wander and to paint their ceremonies, dances, and scenes of their everyday life. On their occasional visits to San Antonio she returned their hospitality by welcoming them to Sunset Hills. Her servants, however, did not always share her pleasure at seeing the Indians. On one visit to San Antonio the Indians learned that Mrs. McNay was ill in a hospital. To leave San Antonio without paying her a courtesy call they considered an unpardonable rudeness, so en masse and wearing their customary Pueblo garments they wandered through the quiet halls of Santa Rosa until they found her room.

In Taos on July 27, 1937, Marion Koogler and Victor Higgins were married. She was then 54 years old and the artist was 53. The marriage was a surprise to mutual friends and most of them, particularly old friends of Higgins, viewed it with considerable misgivings. But Marion Koogler sincerely believed that it would bring happiness to both of them. They had a great deal in common.

Higgins, a talented and recognized artist, had gone to New Mexico in 1914 with a commission to paint the New Mexican landscape from Carter Harrison, art patron and one-time mayor of Chicago. Although he never returned to Chicago to live, Higgins exhibited there annually and was a consistent award winner. One of his better-known paintings, *Winter Funeral,* now owned by the Harwood Foundation of Taos, won both the 1932 First Altman Award of the National Academy of Design and the French Memorial Gold Medal of the Chicago Art Institute.

But the honors and awards had not materially increased Higgins' financial condition and in 1937 he found aesthetic expression seriously handicapped by the pressure of debts. Despite this harassment, he had that year painted his sensitive *Indian Composition,* now in the collection of Mr. and Mrs. Saul Harberg of Taos, which some critics considered proof of his artistic maturity and believed indicated a break with his academic past.

Marion Koogler thought that she could provide the impetus and incentive which would carry Higgins onward from this point in his career to the success which she thought he merited. If she could not herself be his inspiration at least she could supply the means. She was certain that freed from financial worries and the pressure of debts Higgins' artistic growth would continue.

At Sunset Hills a splendid studio was outfitted for his use. In addition to providing a background in which Higgins' creativeness could expand, she assumed all financial obligations, even paying rent on his Taos home and studio, giving his daughter Joan a monthly allowance (on the face of the checks the donor usually wrote: "With lots of love from Mother Marion"), and paying her account at Bullock's Wilshire in Los Angeles. Higgins also had a liberal account in a special bank fund called the Marion and Victor Higgins Household Account. Her other accounts, funds, stocks, and bonds were kept in the name of Marion Koogler McNay.

Mutual friends from Taos were frequent guests at Sunset Hills and during the spring following their marriage the Higginses' guest was Andrew Dasburg, who at that time was ailing from Addison's disease which had seriously interrupted his own successful career. But the friendship between the three which had been so harmonious in the congenial atmosphere of Taos seemed to wither and die at Sunset Hills. The visit and friendship ended abruptly with Marion Koogler paying Dasburg's fare back to Taos. Subsequently she disposed of his paintings in her collection, one of which was *Guaymas, Mexico,* which she had owned since before 1932.

The Higginses' separation on June 15, 1939, was replete with bitterness and recrimination. Marion Koogler went on an extended tour of the western states while Higgins remained in San Antonio and the following November she filed for a divorce in Nevada. Meanwhile Higgins had filed for divorce in San Antonio charging cruelty and alleging that she had interfered with his painting and creative work and asking for his one-half of the community property. Marion Koogler's own petition filed in San Antonio courts charged that Higgins had attempted to conform her to his manners and customs which were alien to those to which she was accustomed.

After the expenditure of considerable legal talent and money a divorce was granted Marion Koogler in San Antonio on March 29, 1940, and her former name restored although she had never ceased to use it during her marriage to Higgins. Again, she found divorce to be an expensive procedure. Higgins returned to Taos and Marion discontinued her annual visits there. The issues of the divorce aroused so much bitterness and animosity among mutual friends that echoes are still heard today. Higgins, however, felt no such rancor. San Antonio artists who studied in Taos during the summers before his death in 1949 were often invited to Higgins' studio in Mabel Dodge Luhan's garden only to be questioned solicitously about Marion Koogler's activities. "She's a great girl!" he frequently told the students.

Higgins' failure was not so much that of a husband as that of an artist. Marion Koogler told friends that he did not paint a single picture during their marriage. She failed to understand how a talent such as his could go stale in the unfamiliar environment which she provided. Afterward, Higgins returned to his former habitat where his artistic productivity noticeably increased and improved. As with his friend Dasburg's painting, Marion Koogler discarded Higgins' *Taos Peak* and *The Gate* which had been shown with her collection at the Witte Museum in 1932.

Seven months after her divorce from Higgins, on October 5, 1940, in Boerne, Texas, Marion Koogler married Adelbert E. Quest, at one time owner of an art gallery in Chicago. She had first met him when he was a partner in the Chester H. Johnson Gallery many years before and in recent years in Taos they had renewed their acquaintanceship. The marriage did not last long enough for Quest to become known to many persons in San Antonio. Those who did meet him recall that he was a likeable person but that he suffered claustrophobia from close confinement at Sunset Hills where his main occupation seems to have been raising chickens. The marriage was fairly miserable for both Marion and Quest and it ended when he returned from a covert visit to Chicago to find his key no longer fit the locks on the doors of Sunset Hills.

Marion Koogler's attempts at conjugal happiness had been expensive but that San Antonio's eventual legacy was so ample is partly due to Dr. Koogler's often repeated admonition not to yield control of her fortune or her business affairs. She heeded his advice and used it as an unalterable guideline throughout her life and was voluble in expressing her gratitude for the lesson her father so indelibly inculcated on her mind.

On the other hand, however, her liberality with friends and relatives and her benevolence to charity, religious and civic organizations were far removed from Dr. Koogler's closefistedness.

Those who knew Marion Koogler in the various phases of her life are frequently in baffling disagreement in their analysis of her personality, but on the subject of her generosity all are in accord. Her method of giving was at times as erratic as her personal relationships. If a friend expressed admiration for one of her possessions, it was likely to be received as a gift on some future anniversary. In gratitude to a surgeon for tending her during a minor operation she urged him to select one of her paintings in addition to his large fee. To another friend she promised a cherished Queen Anne desk he admired but she neglected to include it in her will.

Once struggling with the wrappings of a silver service intended as a present to a priest who had commented on its fine workmanship, she decided to give him something less difficult to wrap. Another time she broke a set of valuable Chinese dog seals used as bookends to give one to the young son of friends but never remembered to give him the mate.

Regardless of the need or personal wealth of her friends Mrs. McNay remembered them and their children and grandchildren, many of whom were her namesakes, with checks or presents on birthdays, anniversaries, and other traditional gift-giving days. She often presented pleasure trips and cruises and expensive automobiles to friends who could well afford to pay for such luxuries themselves and paid pressing debts, financed weddings and college educations for those who could not. She once bought a round-trip ticket to Holland for Marie Esser, a niece of the late Archbishop Drossaerts, who had expressed a longing to have a final visit with her ailing and aged parents.

Every single act of simple kindness or common courtesy whether extended by a friend, a stranger, servant, delivery boy, policeman, waiter, or a sales clerk was certain to be repaid a hundredfold. In-

Marion Koogler McNay, early photograph

variably, her gifts, often lavishly and impulsively bestowed, were merely tangible expressions of an almost pathetic gratitude. She had a charming if unconventional way of writing tenderly affectionate personal messages on gift checks and her thanks and appreciation for special services when paying a bill or a traffic ticket.

Her household servants were always assured of extra pay on birthdays and at Christmas and Easter. A family illness or a personal injury or a hard luck story usually brought additional gratuities and in many cases she paid hospital and medical bills and funeral expenses. In the case of Marcellous C. Armstrong, her long-time butler, major-domo, and friend, her liberality extended to his mother, brother, and even to his church.

Nor was her bounty limited merely to money. On a motor trip to New Mexico her Negro chauffeur became mortally ill in Albuquerque and when immediate professional help was not available Mrs. McNay herself nursed and cared for him in a motel room in a futile effort to save his life.

A number of old friends and family connections were constant recipients of her remembrance. One was Mrs. Addie McNay, the mother of Don Denton McNay, who when she died in 1946 was buried by the side of her son in the beautifully landscaped Koogler lot in Marion, Ohio. After the death of Fleet McNay, her first husband's brother, his widow Elsie Whitney McNay and son Don made their home at Sunset Hills. Mrs. Elsie McNay was her confidential secretary, a position she filled with tactful discretion. Young Don Denton McNay grew up at Sunset Hills and later was a Marine captain. During World War II he trained at Camp Joseph E. Johnston in Florida where the first Don Denton McNay was stationed in World War I.

Another sister-in-law, Mrs. Alta Phillips, her son Robert of Marion, and the Lippincott and Koogler connections, particularly Aunt Clara Lippincott and daughter

Mildred Hamilton who lived in the old Koogler home in Marion, were others who benefited by Mrs. McNay's generosity.

Contributions were almost boundless in the field of organized charities, churches of all denominations, civic, fraternal, political and cultural organizations, and memorial funds. Sometimes these were made in memory of a friend or an event. On a check to the Central Relief Committee for the Unemployed, dated December 9, 1932, Marion Koogler wrote: "In memory of December 9, 1917, Don Denton McNay." That date was the fifteenth anniversary of her marriage, a day she never forgot.

From 1939, Mrs. McNay's most frequent and bountiful contributions were to Roman Catholic organizations and to individual clergymen of the Church.

From girlhood when her Protestant parents had forbidden her marriage to a Catholic, Marion Koogler had had an almost compulsive though secret curiosity about the Catholic Church. This interest intensified as she grew older, and in the traditionally Catholic city of San Antonio she became an active and no longer secret supporter of the Church and eventually a convert. Her greatest patronage and support went to the struggling Missionary Servants of Christ the Master and St. Anthony.

The Servants was a lay society of Catholic women working among the poverty-stricken Mexican Catholics in the community of the Shrine of St. Anthony de Padua. The neighborhood was known as Cementville because of a near-by cement plant where many of the men of the families worked. The Missionary Servants was organized with the approval of the late Archbishop A. J. Drossaerts of San Antonio and under the sponsorship of Reverend Peter M. Baque, a Catalonian, who from 1925 until his death in 1938 was pastor of St. Peter Prince of Apostles Church in San Antonio.

The assistance of the Sisterhood, devoted to teaching and to social work, had been sought by Father Baque when the Mexicans of Cementville resisted his efforts to establish a church among them. The sodality had little success until Mrs. Eugenia Olivier Edwards was accepted as matron. She was then sixty years of age, the mother of eleven children, the grandmother of eighteen, and the great-grandmother of six. Eventually, Mrs. Edwards became Mother Superior of the order she established and was called Mother Theresa. The order received apostolic approval in 1956.

Marion Koogler first met Father Baque when he came to Sunset Hills to visit the family of one of the Mexican gardeners. She was sketching on the grounds when he drove up in his ancient automobile and stopped to ask directions. Mrs. McNay invited him in and over coffee the conversation was devoted to Father Baque's account of the work at the Shrine. It is possible that Father Baque would never have pursued the friendship except for their second meeting. This came one day when he walked into the Shrine and was surprised to find Marion Koogler there. Even then he might have walked away quietly but for the fact that she appeared troubled and disturbed. Father Baque's spiritual guidance resulted in Mrs. McNay's baptism on the feast day of the Virgin of Guadalupe, December 12, 1937, while she was a patient in the Santa Rosa Hospital.

Just before Father Baque's death on February 3, 1938, he turned over to the Missionary Servants a check from Mrs. McNay and told Mother Theresa: "When a founder dies, there is always an angel to care for the order. I believe this lady is destined to be that angel."

Mrs. McNay did indeed become that angel and she never relaxed efforts to fulfill her promise to Father Baque to look after the Sodality after his death. Included in her promise were the Missionary Sisters' St. Anthony Day Nursery, Social Center, and their Home for Working Mexican Girls. During their long friendship Mother Theresa became Marion Koogler's spiritual mother and she was given personal checks on birthdays and on Mother's Days. Although the money was intended for Mother Theresa's private needs, which were great, the devoted Mother always turned it over to the Missionary Servants.

The present Mother Mary John, Sister Rosario, and Sister Genevieve were at the mission during Marion Koogler's lifetime. They remembered with eternal thanksgiving that monthly checks from Mrs. McNay relieved their dire circumstances and actual hunger after Father Baque's death. At one time several new sisters were to take the veil but there were no living quarters available for them at the Shrine. Mrs. McNay provided a dormitory by purchasing two abandoned real estate offices, moving them to the Shrine, and combining them into one building.

Soon after Mother Mary John arrived at the mission in January, 1944, to assume her duties as a Sister, she attended a party at Sunset Hills honoring five new novices. Sunset Hills was covered with a rare snowfall. She remembers that each guest took a turn sitting in a chair which Mrs. McNay called "Father Baque's" because it was the one he occupied when he called on her. One of the novices was the present Sister Genevieve.

In return for Marion Koogler's unfailing kindness, the only gesture of appreciation the Sisters could make was to take fresh buttermilk and home-churned butter from their dairy to Sunset Hills. Invariably, after depositing their dairy products in the kitchen, the Sisters went into the entrance hall to pay homage to El Greco's *Head of Christ*.

The El Greco retained its place among the Modern French masters despite frequent urging by her then husband Victor Higgins and some of his artist friends that it be replaced by an important Impressionist painting. Marion Koogler resisted and held firm to the opinion that her excellent example of the work of El Greco, consid-

ered by many art historians to be the first master of modern art, belonged in her collection and under no condition would she part with it.

However, Mrs. McNay's opposition to Higgins' goading was probably due to an entirely different reason. For it was under the El Greco that an altar was set up each time a priest visited Sunset Hills to administer communion. Mrs. McNay was by then a recluse, so the Church came to her.

Nor did Marion Koogler forget Father Baque. Annually she made contributions in his memory on his feast day and in 1946 she commissioned Charles Umlauf, a talented Texas sculptor, to execute a fourteen-foot aluminum crucifix on a black granite base to be placed at the head of Father Baque's grave in the cemetery of the Sisters of St. Anthony, as the Missionary Servants were known after receiving papal approbation.

Mrs. McNay had met Charles Umlauf, trained at the Chicago Art Institute and an instructor in the art department of The University of Texas, at the opening of his first Texas exhibition at the Witte Museum in 1941 when he shared honors with Everett Spruce, a painting instructor at the University. From this exhibition she purchased several terra cotta figures by Umlauf and a painting by Spruce.

One of Umlauf's pieces, *Christ and the Children*, was shown in plaster. It had been accepted for the Metropolitan Museum of Art's Artists for Victory Exhibition but Umlauf could not afford to have it cast in stone. Umlauf's problem offered Marion Koogler the chance she always welcomed of aiding a talented artist achieve his proper status. She solved it with her customary wholeheartedness by paying for two stone castings of the piece. One was shown in the 1942 Artists for Victory exhibit at the Metropolitan and was included in a smaller version of the same exhibition at the Chicago Art Institute. Later it was purchased by Mrs. McNay and her friend, Mrs. Olivia Nolte, and presented to the Witte Museum.

Mrs. McNay presented the second casting to the Santa Barbara, California, Museum of Art.

The Artists for Victory exhibition was Umlauf's first national showing and it marked the beginning of his highly successful career as a sculptor. In the ensuing years Mrs. McNay continued to be Umlauf's friend and generous patron. The artist remembered with deep gratitude her rare capacity for showing at all times a respect and appreciation for the individuality of an artist.

"She always had the sympathy of the artist at hand because she herself was an artist," Umlauf recalled. "She never, for example, tried to change my work nor to make suggestions that would reflect her own ideas rather than mine. She was a marvelous person to work for, never critical. At the time in my career when I really needed help and encouragement she was there. Mrs. McNay was one of the finest persons I have ever known and had the pleasure of working with. Our acquaintance came at a most important time in my life."

Umlauf was granted a Guggenheim Fellowship in 1949 for which Marion Koogler wrote a recommendation the sculptor remembers as a "wonderful commentary on my work—she was always my champion." In 1960 when his *Reclining Figure II* was awarded a purchase prize by the Ford Foundation, Umlauf named the McNay Art Institute as the recipient of the sculpture.

At one time Marion Koogler considered presenting a sculpture of St. Anthony of Padua, San Antonio's patron saint, to the city for placing in one of its municipal parks. Umlauf submitted several studies, one of which in terra cotta she purchased for her own garden. But for some reason

Left—Texas sculptor Charles Umlauf and assistant install his *Crucifixion* October 16, 1949, at Shrine of St. Anthony

Right—Marion Koogler McNay photographed at a party at her Sunset Hills home

Mrs. McNay changed her mind about the gift to the city and decided instead to commission a large crucifix for the Shrine of St. Anthony.

The *Crucifixion* selected by her was a full-length, elongated and emaciated figure of a suffering Christ but one whose head is joyfully lifted in triumph. She purchased three aluminum castings of a small study, similar but not a duplicate. Two remain in the Museum Collection and the third, originally given to the Susan B. Allen Memorial Hospital in El Dorado, is presently in St. Joseph's Catholic Hospital at Wichita, Kansas. The El Dorado hospital, incidentally, was a memorial to Marion Koogler's mother's old friend, a gift to the town of El Dorado from her son Frank Allen. Mrs. McNay equipped one of the operating rooms as a memorial to Dr. Koogler and commissioned the artist Anthony De Young to paint Mrs. Allen's portrait which presently hangs in the hospital's main entrance.

While the crucifix was in progress, Umlauf and his wife and children were frequent visitors to Sunset Hills and often were present at the Hatfield "unveilings." Umlauf was invariably impressed by Mrs. McNay's spontaneous perception of the merits or shortcomings of the paintings shown. "She had a real firm mind of her own and no one could change it," Umlauf recalled.

The *Crucifixion* was cast in aluminum in New York and Sunday, October 17, 1948, was selected as the date of the dedication.

The day before the ceremony Umlauf and his assistant worked hours in a blazing sun placing the sculpture on its black granite base at the head of Father Baque's grave. The next day the capricious Texas weather changed rapidly and the sun-burned sculptor shivered in falling sleet and a merciless wind as he watched his first monumental piece blessed by the Archbishop of San Antonio.

Among the spectators that day was Ralph M. Pearson, a guest professor of art education at The University of Texas. He reported the event for *Art Digest* and later included his impression of the dedication in *The Modern Renaissance in American Art* (Harper and Brothers, 1954). He wrote:

"If there were seismograph installations distributed among key centers of Western society which would catch and record the vibrations of significant events in art as present instruments respond to earthquake shocks, these new instruments, if they were sensitive enough, would have been set vibrating in many countries by a ceremony which occurred on a cold, windy hilltop in the outskirts of San Antonio, Texas. . . . The event was the dedication of a statue of the Crucifixion by Charles Umlauf, at the Shrine of St. Anthony, donated by Marion Koogler McNay and unveiled and blessed by the Archbishop of San Antonio, His Excellency the Most Reverend Robert E. Lucey.

"History was repeating itself in this dedication of a Crucifix, as history has a way of doing; many a statue of Christ on the Cross has been dedicated on many a hilltop in the past nineteen hundred years. But the things which make this event important and mark it as a carrying on of the supreme achievements of religous art are the facts that it grew honestly and unpretentiously out of the soil of its own community and that the triumvirate of necessary contributing factors to significant production were present.

"There was the generous, informed, and courageous patron. There was an outstanding local artist imbued with a full realization of the profundity and historical continuity of the modern creative renaissance and equipped with the technical mastery of his conception. And finally, the element of need, of usefulness, was present. The Shrine of Saint Anthony serves a settlement of under-privileged Mexican-American workers for whom their Catholic religion is not only the protective mother but also their only release from a hard, grinding materialism into the life of the spirit.

"The Umlauf statue achieves that rare blending of the real and the ideal which marks the perfect symbol. This is not the tortured, suffering, individual man. It is crucified spirit inhabiting Man. It is the drama of the Christian story standing for all human suffering and sacrifice. The art of designed form universalizes the story, turning it into drama. The idea, the ideal, transcends the flesh. The dull-rich gray of the silver-aluminum metal on its black granite base enhances this detachment from the physical. The position on the crest of a low swelling hill seems to echo the delicate balances of meaning and form; this Christ is close to earth and living men, yet not earthbound.

"It was the vision and strong conviction of the late Mrs. Marion McNay which caused this work of art to be produced. Herself an artist and collector of French modern paintings, she was devoting her life, her fortune, and about half of her large, rambling house (in which she endowed a flourishing art school) to bringing a living art to her home city of San Antonio. She keenly enjoyed the constructive experience of initiating the plan for this crucifix, of knowing it would be of profound value to the Church, of commissioning a sculptor in whose work she had confidence, and of helping by consultation (but not dictation) in the planning. By doing these things she was making cultural history, instead of only worshipping at its shrine. She was participating instead of only collecting.

"The vibratory significance of this event reaches far beyond the merits of the one specific work. It lies in the fact that liturgical art is here, again in our time, returning to the grand tradition of creative art."

The afternoon of the dedication a sudden howling Texas norther blew in, bringing threats of a tornado in the rolling and boiling dark clouds that grew momentarily blacker.

"It was as though the hand of God reached down to us," the present Mother Mary John of the Sisters of St. Anthony, at that time a nun, recalled.

"The scene was like a painting by El Greco," Umlauf remembered. "It was bitter cold, all slate gray and black and windy. The robes of the nuns and of the priests were blown about by the wind. Although a great number of people stood about and, it seemed to me, the entire San Antonio police force was there in uniform, it was strangely quiet. Altogether, it was rather eerie. I looked at Mrs. McNay and she looked at me across the crowd and we both smiled. But I saw tears in her eyes, and I think I shed a few tears myself."

Mrs. McNay's dining table

III. THE BEST YEARS

Until 1942 Marion Koogler's collecting had been without plans for either perpetuity or for disposal after her death. She enjoyed thinking of herself as a business woman engaged in the investment field and she once gave this as her occupation on an income tax return. Art was one of the more delightful commodities in which she invested her income. Both her art dealer and her banker considered her astute in her investments. And truly her investment in art was wise and her judgment sound.

Many of her art purchases, as she often pointed out with considerable pride to visitors, had doubled or tripled in value over their original prices.

Naturally, a woman in sole possession of such wealth and with no descendants would draw her share of sycophants who were always free with suggestions or hopes for the disposition of her treasures. Marion Koogler had an uncanny way of eliminating such persons and their advice. But the formidable and often difficult Mrs. McNay failed to deter plans for the disposition of her treasures made by a woman whose persistence and doggedness matched her own. She was Mrs. Ellen Quillin who, almost singlehandedly and in the face of impossible odds, had founded and developed the city's Witte Memorial Museum, which stands as Mrs. Quillin's own monument in San Antonio. In her quiet, deliberate, and penetrating way and with indomitable determination not to lose sight of her goal, Mrs. Quillin launched a campaign to convince Marion Koogler that San Antonio should have a fine arts museum and that she, Marion, should provide it.

On March 2, 1942, Ellen Quillin had paid her usual afternoon visit to Marion Koogler and, as usual, had brought up the subject of converting Sunset Hills into an art center. Again, she was turned down and, undaunted by repeated failure, walked out the door and onto the front terrace but not out of range of Mrs. McNay's firm and husky voice repeating: "No, Ellen. It can't be done! It can't be done!"

The Hatfields were in San Antonio en route to Los Angeles from their annual buying trip and that morning had stopped at Sunset Hills to show their new acquisitions. Mrs. McNay was particularly impressed by an unfinished landscape by Cezanne, *Houses on a Hill (Au Bords du Rivier, Montaigne, St. Victoria)*, an oil in soft blues and greens with exposed areas of white canvas. But, she explained to the Hatfields, due to commitments outside the field of art, she did not feel that she could afford it.

In the afternoon, while Mrs. Quillin was visiting Sunset Hills, Dalzell Hatfield was in his hotel room packing the Cezanne and other paintings for shipment to Dallas. After the crates had been delivered to the Railway Express office, the Hatfields returned to Sunset Hills for dinner.

Ruth Hatfield remembered the evening as an exceedingly pleasant occasion and that Marion's exuberant and witty conversation kept the guests at the table until almost midnight. Mrs. Hatfield recalled: "Suddenly, and in the middle of a sentence on an unrelated subject, Marion exclaimed as though the idea had most unexpectedly and not until that moment occurred to her: 'Now I know what to do with the collection when I pass on; now I see what I've been building toward all these years. A museum of modern art!—one of the first in America, and these paintings will form the nucleus of that collection.'

"I had never seen her so happy, nor so thrilled, and in her excitement Marion talked on for an hour or more, seldom pausing, outlining her plans for a museum, the additions she would need for her collection, and the conversion of her house into an art museum. We realized then that the problem of disposing of the collection and her home after her death had been for some time a matter of great concern to her.

"Now she had the solution, and at last knew why, as a girl, she had insisted on going to the Art Institute of Chicago to study. The segments of her life now formed a pattern which revealed the purpose of her life and she was at long last content.

"Our conversation that night was a culmination of many previous talks over a number of years. At various times Marion considered leaving her paintings to the National Gallery, to the Museum of Modern Art, or to the Chicago Art Institute. On all these occasions, Dal advised her that those museums already had important collections of modern French art and that hers would be only a small section in any of them, but that if she gave them to San Antonio the gift would be an eternal monument to her good taste and to her lifelong interest in art. He pointed out that leaving the collection to San Antonio in the final analysis would benefit the whole art world of America, for all time to come. Thus, we too were happy at her decision. I am sure that Mrs. Quillin also, whenever Marion talked about this matter, advised her to leave the collection in San Antonio. Mrs. Quillin, I must say, has done a magnificent job on her own, and I remember the days when Mrs. Drought, Ellen, and Eleanor Onderdonk kept the fires of art burning with a

courage against great odds that were monumental.

"We didn't leave Sunset Hills until two o'clock in the morning and we had just gone to sleep in our hotel when, about four o'clock, the telephone rang. It was Marion. She apologized for calling at that hour and explained that she was too excited to sleep. And, since she was planning to found a museum of modern art she felt that Cezanne, the father of modern French art, must be represented. Would we please bring back the Cezanne!"

Without revealing the fact that Cezanne at that moment was well on the way to Dallas, the Hatfields assured her they would bring it the following evening when they came for dinner. What followed was probably only routine in the life of an art dealer. By 6 a.m., Mr. Hatfield had arranged to have the crate containing the Cezanne landscape removed from the train when it arrived at Waco and placed on the next train back to San Antonio. The painting was uncrated in the Express office and hand-delivered at Sunset Hills before dinner.

Mrs. Quillin was another who received a telephone call early on the morning of March 3, 1942. Marion Koogler's voice vibrated with excitement and determination when she made the announcement: "Ellen! I'm going to do it!" and for several hours Ellen Quillin listened with intense relief and with some degree of self-satisfaction as Marion Koogler unfolded her plans for a center of modern art.

Immediately Marion Koogler took the first step in her plans for a center of art at Sunset Hills—a school of art. Since 1939 she had been a patron and a member of the Witte Museum School of Art, sponsored by the Art League, which was scheduled to close due to wartime difficulties. Her offer of school space in a steel-framed aviary now converted into a roomy skylighted studio at Sunset Hills was most gratefully accepted by the directors.

On March 31, 1942, school directors

called a meeting at Sunset Hills and invited city and chamber of commerce officials to hear Marion Koogler's future plans to bequeath her home, collection, the proposed school, and an endowment to the city of San Antonio. She asked that no publicity be given the project.

The minutes of the meeting record that "Mrs. McNay's offer was so magnanimous all were breathless for a few minutes. . . . the Board adjourned still unable to project themselves fully into a school set-up where the worries of housing and maintenance would be comparatively light. It was one of the great moments in the lives of those privileged to be present."

Among the school board members present was the late Dr. Frederic G. Oppenheimer, whose collection of Flemish and Gothic art was housed in a private museum at his residence. Although there was marked contrast in their taste in art Mrs. McNay and Dr. Oppenheimer were the only serious and astute art collectors at that time in San Antonio. Appropriately, he was called upon to say a few words on the occasion and his reply is long remembered for its brevity and conciseness: "Mrs. McNay, you have stolen my thunder." Eventually the two diverse collections of the old friends would blend together in Mrs. McNay's museum.

The San Antonio Art Institute opened in the fall of 1942 in the former aviary back of Mrs. McNay's residence. It continued under the sponsorship of the Art League and the direction of the late Charles Rosen. Rosen and his wife, who became the Institute's librarian, were assigned an apartment in the main house.

School operations were no longer restricted to tuition fees but were considerably boosted by financial assistance from Mrs. McNay. She paid maintenance costs, models' fees, advertising and printing expenses; provided living quarters for guest instructors and directors; and met the deficit in salaries and travel expenses. The big house at Sunset Hills was opened for group meetings, social events for students and faculty, benefits, lecture tours of the collection, and musicals.

Marion Koogler materially added to her private library for use of the school until it equalled that of many Texas public and university art book collections. Additionally, she accumulated a wealth of the finest and rarest reproductions available. The library, as well as the painting collection, was open to students and teachers.

Despite an almost morbid reluctance to view the passing of time realistically, the last few years of Mrs. McNay's life were rewarding ones. She abandoned her futile search for personal happiness and subjugated her private life in the interest of founding an art center. She rarely left Sunset Hills.

A description of the Marion Koogler of later years was provided by Ruth Hatfield: "The first five or six years we knew her, she was slender and quite regal in appearance and wore utterly beautiful clothes. After she became heavier, she started wearing the peasant dresses that were extremely becoming to her. Their white and pastel colors and hand embroidery around the low necks were very becoming. Her hair was still dark and she had beautiful skin and extremely expressive eyes. Her eyes spoke for her—they could sparkle with humor, fill with compassion and sympathy, indicate disgust about things she did not approve, and beam with love and approbation at other times. While one might not have thought her beautiful from the standpoint of the beauty of a motion picture star, she had the everlasting beauty of a woman like Katharine Cornell."

Quietly and with the invaluable assistance and constant encouragement of the Hatfields, Marion Koogler directed her art purchases toward a definite goal—a collection which would exemplify the development of modern art.

Rouault's *Christ and the Disciples*, a Dufy oil, and an exquisite watercolor by Demuth were among the additions in 1943.

Marie Laurencin's *In the Forest* and Andre Dunoyer de Segonzac's *Trees,* both oils, joined the collection in 1944.

In the following years the collection grew to magnificent proportions with the inclusion of Modigliani's *Girl With Blue Eyes,* Picasso's *Girl With Plumed Hat* and *Guitar and Wine Glass,* Pisarro's *Haymakers Resting,* Redon's *Profile and Flowers,* Matisse's *The Red Blouse,* and Cezanne's *Portrait of Dr. Henri Gasquet.*

For the acquisition of *Dr. Gasquet,* Mrs. McNay expanded her picture budget far beyond the customary range by paying $34,000 for the superb canvas, but in the years ahead its minimum value would exceed $300,000.

The periodic visits of the Hatfields to show new acquisitions were events open to students, the faculty, and members of the Art League. Mrs. McNay invited certain prosperous San Antonians to these viewings in a deliberate attempt to stimulate their feeble interest in art into active collecting. She ardently hoped that others would become habitual collectors of modern art and that their collections would someday be added to the holdings of her proposed museum. Although her plan was not altogether successful it is likely that her efforts initiated later collecting.

Crates of paintings were unpacked by Mr. Hatfield in the reception hall. Marion Koogler sat in her customary straight-back chair while students and other guests found places on the floor and on the steps of the grand staircase. Such an exhibition of the world's greatest masters was a rare opportunity in those days in Texas.

The occasions were made even more privileged by an informal critique by two authorities—Mrs. McNay and Dalzell Hatfield. But when the discussion was over and the pictures back in their crates, the audience was always in doubt as to which paintings Mrs. McNay preferred.

Mrs. Hatfield described the final moments of decision: "When Marion actually came to the point of deciding what she would buy only she, Dal, and I were present. On rare occasions Elsie was there. Usually, after we had shown the paintings and had dined with Marion and were back in our hotel for the evening, Marion would telephone and talk to Dal about various paintings. The conversations between Marion and Dal were on a scholarly basis. Then Marion usually made her final decision the following day. There is no doubt that Dal influenced her tremendously in her collecting, but as one scholar would influence another."

Board members and the faculty often found that Mrs. McNay was not available for conference but she always found time to listen to the painting and personal problems of students. She frequently substituted as a teacher and regularly lectured on color and composition and conducted unscheduled critiques of students' work. She encouraged them in their art by purchasing their paintings and offering awards, prizes, and scholarships to the Art Institute of Chicago. From one annual school exhibition she bought twelve paintings. Many of these purchases of students' and teachers' work were given away to friends or to art museums.

Most of the students were unaware that Mrs. McNay's sharp eyes were constantly on their work, searching hopefully for indications of unusual talent among them. Max Fitzpatrick, now a successful artist working in San Francisco, remembered the day he was called from Buckley Mac-Gurrin's class by Mrs. Elsie McNay who explained that Mrs. McNay wanted to see him. Fitzpatrick was astonished that he was even known to Mrs. McNay. She was ill and Fitzpatrick was taken to her bedroom for his first and only conversation with her. He recalled their general discussion of art, her witty remarks, and her words to him: "Well, young man, it looks like I have found another scholarship to the Chicago Art Institute." He returned to class somewhat stunned and the remainder of the session was taken up by the students' excited comments on Mrs. McNay's interest in struggling artists. Fitzpatrick probably would have been another beneficiary of a scholarship but Mrs. McNay's death occurred a short while after her interview with him.

Among the few student paintings which Marion Koogler did *not* give away and which remains in the Museum Collection is one purchased off an easel in Etienne Ret's class. It is a delicately beautiful watercolor, *Mother and Child*, painted by Mrs. Ruth Dunn. Periodically, Mrs. McNay visited classes and observed students at work. On one such visit in 1946 she stood behind Mrs. Dunn and after watching her paint for awhile said: "That's nice. What do you want for it?"

"I was overwhelmed," Mrs. Dunn recalled. "I felt I should pay her. And, of course, I was terribly pleased because in my opinion she had a flawless taste in art and an infallible eye. Listening to her discussion and explanation of the paintings in her collection and those exhibited for her consideration by the Hatfields was a rare privilege. Mrs. McNay made art appear to be like the highest soaring of wings. Attending the Art Institute was a great experience. Everything was on such a grand scale. I shall always remember the GI bill boys tripping over fine Oriental rugs every afternoon when Armstrong appeared at the curb in the long black limousine to drive them to their required commercial classes in Brackenridge Park. But above all I remember the inspiration created by Mrs. McNay. Even in the old pongee house coat and tennis shoes she was very much the *grande dame*."

Ruth Dunn gave up a successful career as a painter for an even greater one as an artist-designer in stained glass. Her work is represented in a number of churches, universities and office buildings.

Another student-painting remaining in the Museum Collection is a watercolor, *Carnival*, done by Jack Tinkle in Dan Lutz's class in 1946. Tinkle was offered a scholarship to Chicago Art Institute by Mrs. McNay but his impending marriage prevented his acceptance. Today one of San Antonio's popular artists, Tinkle recalled Mrs. McNay as a "real wonderful person."

There was a succession of directors, guest instructors, and teachers at the Art Institute, many of them recommended by the Hatfields.

Dorothy Johnson Bergamo, instructor in painting and in the history of art from 1943 through 1945, lived at Sunset Hills with her son Ronald while her husband Ralph was stationed at one of the army bases.

Dan Lutz, the talented California painter, was engaged for the 1946 season and when he became ill was replaced by Etienne Ret, a native of France, who came from the staff of the Chouinard School of Art. Ret, whose oil *First Son* is in the present Museum Collection, brought a new approach to local painting which was heartily endorsed by Mrs. McNay. Regionalism was noticeably lacking in his painting but it was his unpardonable act of eliminating the popular Tom Lea from a Texas show he juried that focused criticism on art which was denounced as "spiritually meaningless to this part of the world." An incisive contemporary appraisal of Mrs. McNay's school was given by Lea's good friend and San Antonio writer Green Peyton in his *The Southwest* (University of Oklahoma Press, 1948):

"A case in point is the San Antonio Art Institute, an academy which is intimately associated with the Witte Museum in San Antonio. Its moving spirit is a rich art patron and collector, Marion Koogler McNay. Mrs. McNay is a graduate of the Art Institute of Chicago who once was a painter herself. She fell in love with the modern French schools, and has devoted her life to their advancement.

"In her expansive colonial Spanish home, on a hilltop northeast of San Antonio, Mrs. McNay has one of the finest private collections of modern French art in existence. It includes at least one work by every Gallic master since Gauguin. Pablo Picasso, Henri Matisse, Toulouse Lautrec, Georges Braque, Paul Cezanne, Modigliani—all these and more rub elbows on Mrs. McNay's walls. At the back of her house are the classrooms of the Art Institute, where students paint reverently in the shadow of these renowned artists.

"To instruct them in the mysteries of her cult, Mrs. McNay imported a minor artist from France. Etienne Ret is a devotee of Georges Rouault, whose darkly colorful canvases look like distorted stained-glass windows. Ret spends three months each year teaching in San Antonio; three months or so in Los Angeles; and the rest of the year in France. . . .

"This same Etienne Ret who instructs Mrs. McNay's pupils not long ago was one of three jurors chosen by the Houston Museum to assemble a traveling exhibition of Texas painters for display throughout the state. Among the works submitted was a handsome oil, *The Shining Plain,* by Tom Lea of El Paso. It showed a pioneer on horseback riding west through a hip-tall waste of grass, so silken that you could feel the wind rustling over it. The picture was rejected. It was a realistic canvas of the sort that is native to this region. The show contained instead a conglomerate collection of cubist, expressionist, abstract, and surrealistic art, weakly imitating the modern French masters. It left most Texans who saw it at all with a justifiable sense of frustration or indifference."

Marion Koogler indicated no concern that the cult she was promoting was endangering good, solid Southwestern art and when Ret decided to visit France she sought another instructor of the same school. Ret was succeeded by Buckley Mac-Gurrin who also came from Chouinard. Presently he is teaching and painting in El Monte, California. Recently he recalled his experience at the San Antonio Art Institute:

"My first contact with Marion McNay was by telephone. She called me at my home in El Monte from San Antonio concerning my appointment as guest instructor at the San Antonio Art Institute. I remember a contralto voice, pleasant, cordial, and humorous, but at the same time dignified and without arrogance. This phone conversation was the closest thing to a contract that ever existed between us.

"I was to succeed my good friend the poet-painter Etienne Ret for the term beginning in February, 1948. With my wife Margot I set off the last couple of days in January in our pre-war convertible which had no heater and only a cloth top. By the time we reached Yuma, Arizona, the temperature had dropped to several degrees below zero, and there it remained until we were well into Texas.

"I had a monumental cold when I met a large class after our arrival at Sunset Hills. Jessie (Lippincott) Winkworth, who became my good right hand, read a message of welcome and introduction from Mrs. McNay. The moment the class was over I returned to our apartment in the McNay house and fell into bed. This routine I repeated for several days, until at length I thawed out and could function more or less normally.

"There was a certain amount of protocol surrounding my first meeting with Marion McNay, as there was indeed with her relations with everyone. She spent by far the greater part of her time in her upstairs quarters of the great house; she very seldom left Sunset Hills for any purpose. (Once when she took us to the Menger Hotel for Christmas dinner she was received like visiting royalty.)

"People generally came to her, by appointment. And so it was when I first met her face to face after we had been on the scene a few days.

"In the big downstairs living room, at right angle to a tall window overlooking the front lawn of the house, was placed a high-backed divan of dark wood and upholstered in maroon velvet. Above it on the gray wall hung one of her favorite paintings: the blue-eyed, red-haired girl in a black sweater by Modigliani. Marion received me seated on this divan, her customary place, I learned. She was wearing one of her many Indian dresses of white linen or cotton, with a bit of colored embroidery here and there. Her hair was not thick, and it was cut very short like a man's haircut. She was quite heavy; her skin was very white and very smooth; her eyes dark, lively, intelligent. I saw her sitting thus, and thus attired, many times thereafter.

"As our friendship developed, she would sometimes come to call. Our apartment was on the north side of the patio, upstairs, opening onto a loggia. Although Marion could have reached it directly from her upstairs quarters by following a gallery and the loggia, she approached from across the patio. And she invariably wore a hat on such occasions. She would spend perhaps an hour, looking at my paintings and talking about art and her experiences in art and life. It was interesting, friendly, amusing, even enlightening talk. She told anecdotes with great humor.

"My first stay in San Antonio ended in June, 1948. We returned for the term beginning in October of that year. We enjoyed the same lovely apartment and the same cordial relationship with Mrs. McNay and Elsie McNay, who had welcomed us so graciously on our first arrival at Sunset Hills, and with the invaluable Jessie Winkworth.

"Marion McNay's ideas concerning the school were clear to me from our close association: her basic idea was to develop, if possible, outstanding artists in the fine arts field. The school was, of course, not a commercial enterprise. Developing creative talent was its purpose. Marion's hope was that as a result of her sponsorship there might emerge some regional work of art which would have status comparable with that which formed her modern French collection. The ideal was the school's *raison d'etre*.

"To this ideal she brought practical vision and plenty of good common sense. The steadfastness of her basic purpose (the discovery and development of superior talent) was clearly reflected in her refusal, in spite of discreet but persistent urging by certain people, to have the school accredited so as to be able to confer degrees in the fine arts—a move which would certainly have attracted additional students, but no doubt students primarily interested in acquiring credentials to become art teachers rather than practicing creative artists.

"But she took the necessary steps to enable the school to enroll ex-service personnel. To satisfy the government's GI bill requirements, she set up the commercial art studio in Brackenridge Park where the bill's beneficiaries could supplement their fine arts training at Sunset Hills with excellent instruction in all aspects of commercial art under Warren Hunter. She was a practical idealist.

"The prestige of the school was dear to Marion McNay. I think she inspired the teachers to give their best. She provided an art library the memory of which still floods me with envy. There was a huge collection of works of art of many periods. Her own fine collection of important modern paintings was always available to our classes. She encouraged the students in many ways: the school's exhibit at the annual River Show was an outstanding event; the school parties she gave helped to integrate the student body which was drawn from various social levels; she sometimes purchased students' works; and to at least two boys in my classes (Chris Gonzalez and Carlos Rios) she gave scholarships to her own Alma Mater, the Chicago Art Institute.

"The satisfaction with my work at the school, which Marion expressed often and clearly, was greatly appreciated by me and I cherished the many indications of her affection for me as a person. But to me, as an artist who does some teaching (rather

Marion Koogler McNay, standing at easel, instructs a painting class in the patio of her residence

"In March, 1949, she commissioned me to do a portrait of her attorney, Mr. Moloney of Marion, Ohio, who prolonged his stay in San Antonio for ten days so that I might execute it. A couple of months later she had me do a portrait of Miss Nancy Russell of San Antonio which she presented to the sitter. Toward the end of the fall term of 1949 she again honored me by proposing that I do a small portrait of her.

"I was particularly touched since she told me that, although she had often during her life been asked to sit to various artists, she had never done so. But to my regret she was unwilling to be painted as she appeared at that time. And so, I was obliged to do her portrait mostly from photographs taken some years before.

"Of course, it was a hard thing to do, but since she was so very sensitive to the marks of age she insisted that the portrait be done as she had appeared some twenty years previously. I regretted this stipulation on her part, not only because it made the work more difficult but because a portrait of her as she appeared in her later years would have meant much more to those who knew her at that time. In my opinion she had a very paintable head with much character. However, I did as she wished. She was highly pleased with the results and put the painting in the living room.

"These successive indications of her interest in my work caused me great pleasure, for I had the greatest esteem for her critical insight and artistic perception.

"I had dinner with Marion on Christmas of 1949. In January she went to the hospital.

"I now had spent the school years from February 1948 through January 1950 at the San Antonio Art Institute. I had enjoyed it and had made many good friends there. But I now felt that I would prefer to spend more time in California. Conse-

than a teacher who does some painting) the esteem she showed for my talent was the source of my greatest satisfaction.

"Thus I felt deeply honored when, in June, 1948, she purchased my painting of the Annunciation called *Angelus Domini* and hung it between the great entrance hall and the dining room, thereby establishing it as a part of the Marion Koogler McNay Collection. Later that month she purchased my small painting called *Recuerdo de Chile* and presented it to the Witte Museum.

52

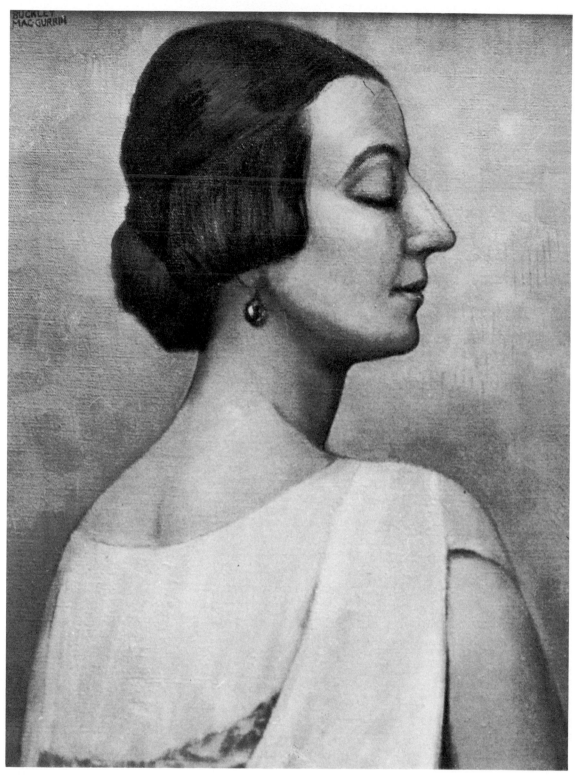

Marion Koogler McNay
Buckley Mac-Gurrin, artist. Collection of the McNay Art Institute

quently it was arranged that Michael Frary would take over the guest instructor post in February, 1950, and that I would return for the fall term of that year.

"My parting with the class at Sunset Hills was a memorable one for me, for between the students and myself there had built up a rapport of sympathy, understanding, and affection—the kind of thing that makes old teachers, if they are lucky enough to have experienced it, grow misty-eyed.

"Before I took the long road for home I stopped by the hospital to say goodbye to Marion. She said many kind things to me; we exchanged jokes and had a fine conversation. It was a delightful visit and we had an affectionate parting. That was the last time I saw this fine woman and beloved friend. In April I was greatly shocked and deeply grieved to hear of her death.

"The grief, the sorrow, and the sense of a rare bright light having gone out that I experienced then, I still feel more than fourteen years later."

Buckley Mac-Gurrin's portrait of Marion Koogler McNay remains in the Museum Collection.

Additionally it contains two sanguine on paper drawings of her likeness by Maude Phelps McVeigh Hutchins. However, the most striking portrait of Mrs. McNay is a delicately beautiful polychromed plaster bust which, according to friends of long standing, is a remarkable likeness of a younger Marion Koogler. The sculptor remains unknown. So far as it can be determined Mrs. McNay never revealed the name of the artist to anyone and it was seldom on display in her house. Some think it was done by a fellow student at the Chicago Art Institute, others believe it to be the work of Mrs. Hutchins, but the most likely assumption is that it is a self-portrait.

Only a few of Mrs. McNay's personal letters are extant, which were written to the Hatfields. Ruth Hatfield most generously provided excerpts from them:

February 2, 1948: "Your full, rich letter and deluxe catalogue, *Eight Masterpieces*, came yesterday and today the two thrilling pictures. You have given me so much to contemplate and think about. But then—the best part of my life, the last few years that I have been building for the future—is all due to your inspiration and help. Without your true friendship and interest I could never have been able to build my collection and carry on the successful art school. Both are fruits of your interest and help. San Antonio can thank the Hatfields for the building of the Collection of truly great pictures and the Art Institute is your baby as much as it is mine. Not many babies have three parents but this live and growing one has. It seems to be two-thirds Hatfield and one-third McNay and a very lively and growing child that partakes generously of the best, I feel, of its three parents. . . . The Utrillo print is a beauty—the finest one I know. It is so rich in color."

February 3, 1948: "The Mac-Gurrins arrived Saturday shortly after lunch. They had a hectic trip—sand storms in the desert and in the mountains and west of El Paso deep snow—with no chains and no heat in the car. They reached El Paso and stayed, I believe, in a poor tourist camp Thursday night, the coldest weather on record there, six below zero. But they took it in their stride and laughed it off as 'experience.' Saturday was one of those perfect days with brilliant sunlight. They loved it. That night it started to rain and has been raining most of the time since. It is the first good rain since the flood nearly a year and a half ago. We have started the school out here full up and almost overflowing. There were a few new students yesterday and three more this morning, thirty-six in all. Jessie [Winkworth] was not going to take the last one, thirty-five being the limit, but Buckley told the girl, a former student, that it would be all right with him. He does not seem afraid of work. Saturday afternoon he came over and asked for suggestions and he is carrying them right out. He made a typewritten program for the next three weeks yesterday and put it on the bulletin board. . . . I am sure that Buckley will be just the one for the school at this time. The students are all quite enthusiastic about him.

"The Mac-Gurrins and Rets had dinner together Saturday night and the Rets left for Mexico, by train, Sunday night. There was a man who came out on Sunday to see the collection who had been down in Mexico and was on his way back to New York. Etienne met him and right away decided they would go to one of the little villages and live in a very primitive way and not spend much money. Said it would be good preparation for Catherine and Stepheny before returning to France. . . .

"The Mac-Gurrins both have had colds caught on their way to Texas. Buckley had a terrible cold and I was quite worried. He spent Tuesday afternoon and all of Wednesday in bed and was able to go down to the studio for awhile yesterday and today (Friday).

"The recent silk screen print by Millard Sheets delights me greatly. The fine rhythm and design, the strong contrasts, and rich harmony of color, the seeming simplicity make for a very handsome and masterful picture. I appreciate its being endorsed by the artist and signed to me. It is a real addition to my collection and I will have it framed soon.

"The Feininger picture [*Summer Clouds*, watercolor, a gift to Mrs. McNay from the Hatfields] wears well and gets better all of the time. One of the instructors in the art department of the University came over from Austin recently just to see our collection. He had spent much time in New York and seemed quite familiar with Feininger's work and said the one you sent me was, he thought, the very best he had ever seen.

"Charles Umlauf stopped in his tracks before he got through the door and exclaimed when he beheld the new Rouault [*The Dancer*]. *Rosalie* [Raoul Dufy] sits

in her corner and beams. She delights me every time I go into the room. Her conduct is perfection. She is a real personality and brings joy and youth into our house."

February 9, 1948: "Mary and Arthur [Hines, Ruth Hatfield's sister and brother-in-law of San Antonio] entertained the Mac-Gurrins and Elsie [McNay] Friday night at the Menger. Elsie reported a fine and lavish dinner, a very jolly time and Mary a very gracious hostess. As I couldn't attend, Mary and Arthur sent me a lovely box of candy.

"Thank you again for the beautiful inlaid box you sent me for my birthday. I do not need it to remind me of my two dearest and best friends but I will keep it near by and love you both.

"The sky is clear and sun shining this morning—first for a week ago Saturday. It went down in the twenties last night.

"Gladys Spencer, the Kansas friend who has come down and stayed with me so many times while Elsie has gone to Ohio, is visiting her sister in Los Angeles and sent a nice clipping about your show and had seen your fine collection of Eight and was loud in her praises. Sincere thanks for all that you have done for me. Best wishes and dearest love always."

Sunset Hills was seldom closed to visitors and never to the many soldiers stationed at San Antonio military bases during the war nor to students.

Ward Lockwood and other instructors from the art department of The University of Texas often brought their classs for a tour of the house.

A young man who often came over from the Mill Race studio class of lithography with Alice Naylor, the instructor, was Paul Wonner who was stationed at one of the military bases. In 1965 on the occasion of a one-man exhibition of his paintings at the Marion Koogler McNay Art Institute, Paul Wonner recalled with great pleasure his wartime studies and visits to Sunset Hills.

Another visitor was the Utah-born artist

Artist Ward Lockwood and Mrs. Lockwood in patio of Sunset Hills with Mrs. McNay

Dean Fausett who was using his 1943 Guggenheim to execute documentary murals at Randolph Air Force Base. He had studied mural painting with Boardman Robinson at the Colorado Springs Fine Arts Center and shared Mrs. McNay's interest in the Southwest. He was impressed by what he termed her "avant-garde mind."

Robert Ardrey, at the time a successful dramatist who was just beginning his own art collection and later became famous for his book *African Genesis*, came to Sunset Hills with Mrs. Florence Rosengren, owner of a bookstore, on a hot July 4th afternoon. After viewing the collection they were served ice cream and cake in the library and Mrs. McNay read aloud a letter just received from Etienne Ret. Mrs. Rosengren cast a brief look at a rare collection of luster and Victorian figurines, presently in the Witte Museum, which was displayed on the mantelpiece and bookcase shelves. Mrs. McNay asked her if she liked them and quickly sensing that Mrs. Rosengren's hesitancy indicated she did not, bluntly remarked: "That's good! Most people admire them at length and ignore the paintings."

The housing shortage and inconveniences of her World War I experiences as a bride in Laredo were never forgotten. When similar conditions prevailed in San Antonio during World War II Mrs. McNay purchased and furnished fifteen rental houses and apartments in the suburbs of San Antonio, added five apartments to the original structure of her home, and moved five other small houses onto the grounds of Sunset Hills.

She planned the remodeling and decorating of each rental unit and herself did much of the manual work and repairs. Once when she was engaged in stippling the floors of one of the houses, a minister seeking a contribution wandered in to ask directions to the main house. After watching her work for awhile he asked: "Do you know Mrs. McNay?" She curtly replied: "I know her *quite* well. But you can't see her now, she's much too busy." She continued working and the minister left without his contribution, never knowing the identity of the paint-smeared woman on the floor.

Sunset Hills soon became a self-contained little colony of congenial and interesting tenants, usually screened and selected for their social qualities. In her self-imposed seclusion, Marion Koogler created her own pleasant world. She proved a most unusual landlady in many ways but more especially because she seldom cashed her tenants' rental checks. After her death this oversight created havoc with the bank accounts of those ten-

ants who could be located when checks, some dating back a number of years, were cashed by the administrator. This source added more than $17,000 to the McNay estate.

Tenants for eight years at Sunset Hills were Mr. and Mrs. Joe Cody who occupied an apartment in the main house. Mrs. Cody first met Mrs. McNay when she came to Sunset Hills to get her approval of an advertisement for the San Antonio Art Institute. Mrs. McNay rejected the ad and said she would rewrite it. Mrs. Cody protested but was firmly told: "I'll write the ad. I'm paying for it."

From this inauspicious beginning a mutually warm friendship developed. Mrs. Cody, a raconteur of note and possessing an unfailing sense of humor, was an appreciative audience for Mrs. McNay's own Rabelaisian wit, droll comments, and anecdotes of her life and of the lives of some of her more distinguished acquaintances.

Mrs. McNay often came by the Codys' apartment at the cocktail hour for there she was certain to find a lively gathering of wits. Next to telling one, she most enjoyed hearing a good story.

Mrs. Cody was editor of a weekly visitors' guide to events in the city and she persuaded Marion Koogler to become a contributor to the "Poesy Department." Her printed poetry covered a wide range of subjects and moods.

Sometimes wearing a man's hat and a mink coat over an old dress, Mrs. McNay could be seen on the grounds sketching Sunset Hills scenes. Her total disinterest in clothes and in her appearance in general disturbed some of her friends but Rose Cody was the only one with the courage to do something about it. Once she saw an especially handsome dress of navy blue with a wide beaded yoke in a downtown dress shop which she thought would be suitable for Mrs. McNay. She impulsively charged it to Mrs. McNay's account and had it delivered on approval. Thinking it over on the way home she was appalled at her presumptuousness and confessed her daring act as soon as she arrived. Far from being offended Mrs. McNay regarded it as a thoughtful gesture and met the challenge by wearing it at a party and enduring the unaccustomed confinement of foundation garments. And, appropriately costumed for the role, Mrs. McNay reached far back in her repertoire and to the delight of her guests put on her old Marie Antoinette Murdock act. The performance over, she put the dress away in a closet full of beautiful gowns of another day and returned to her favorite loose shifts. She was buried in the dress Rose Cody bought.

When Marion Koogler was too ill to greet visitors the duty of hostess was performed by Elsie McNay. Frequently ill and depressed she withdrew from all contact and for long periods remained in her room. Her only companion during these times was the devoted Elsie McNay who read aloud for endless hours. Mrs. McNay had suffered an eye hemorrhage in the early 1930's which gradually weakened the sight of one eye.

As she had done since early childhood, Marion Koogler found refuge from reality in bed and during these times nothing could induce her to leave it, not even when the bed itself collapsed from sheer weariness of its burden. When this happened she remained prone on the mattress and left the problem of righting the bed with her in it to the harassed and faithful butler Armstrong.

In these prolonged periods of depression she was usually attended by Dr. Merton M. Minter, presently a patron of the arts whose interest first developed under the tutelage of his patient. As a therapeutical device to stir her out of lethargy Dr. Minter's deliberately critical and unflattering remarks about one of her paintings would bring an immediate response. And for the next hour or so the doctor listened to her analysis of the painting he had belittled. The therapy worked both ways. It could

hardly have been a coincidence that many years later as chairman of the Board of Regents of The University of Texas Dr. Minter nominated Charles Umlauf as the sculptor of major pieces for the campus and new University buildings.

Mrs. McNay's bed in later years became a sanctuary, a place of retreat. One who understood Mrs. McNay's deep need for meditation was Mrs. Hatfield. She explained:

"Marion's going to bed for various lengths of time really gave her time for her most creative and productive ideas. Always after she had been in bed for a week, two weeks, or just two days, she would come forth bubbling with new ideas, with decisions accomplished and, additionally, she would have enlarged and increased her knowledge in certain fields of art. Sometimes she would also have analyzed a problem or a person's motive. Therefore, during all the time we knew her, the last sixteen years of her life, these periods of contemplation were exceedingly valuable.

"One of Marion's greatest characteristics was her supreme self-confidence in her own decisions. Her periods of staying in bed brought her to decisions that in almost all cases proved to be absolutely correct. Her decisions about matrimony seem to be errors which some very wealthy women often make. The one thing they want which in some cases they cannot have is a happy marriage."

These self-imposed retreats were lonely days for Marion Koogler and it was during one of them that she wrote:

"A friend passed by one day
And tossed a peach seed 'neath my
   window sill.
May be he never came this way again
And never will.
I'm sure he did not know
The seed would grow.
He does not know I think of him as
   'friend.'

A spring graduation fiesta was an annual event for students and faculty
of the San Antonio Art Institute.

A Christmas party for students and their families in the big central hall
of Sunset Hills was traditional.

Yet when the south winds bend
The tree tops and the brown buds swell,
I'd like to tell
Him all this tree
Has meant to me.
I used to sally forth to meet the spring,
I searched for her on hill, in field,
    through glen.
Again spring comes.

The mystery—
The first pink promise, then
The miracle of bloom
Outside my room.
I wish my friend, wherever he may be
Could see our tree."

The peach tree of which she wrote and for whose blossoms she waited with such eagerness each new spring still grows. Second-floor gallery visitors in the spring share Mrs. McNay's pleasure at the sight of the delicate pink blossoms framed by one of the windows.

Social events at Sunset Hills were centered around school activities. Three annual parties became traditional: Mrs. McNay's birthday on February 7, a graduation fiesta in the patio on May 20, and a Christmas gathering.

The birthday observance, which the Museum continues as Founders Day, began in 1944 as a surprise party arranged by board members and Mrs. McNay's good friends, Mrs. Vernon Taylor, Mrs. Atlee B. Ayres, and Mrs. Olivia Nolte. On that day Mrs. Lutcher Brown brought a lei of camellias from her gardens at Oak Court, and placed them around Mrs. McNay's neck, a gesture which in itself became traditional. Mrs. McNay's last birthday party was in 1950 and, although desperately ill, she came downstairs for a brief visit. It was her last public appearance.

The graduation fiesta was a gay and colorful patio event when most of the guests came in costume. In honor of the occasion Mrs. McNay composed a song, *Chiquita*, which became the party's theme.

At Christmas an enormous tree was placed in the center of the entrance hall. Children of students and the faculty were included and a belief in Santa Claus was doubtless prolonged by the convincing role played by artist George Baylous. Guests filled the entrance hall and the stairway while he handed out gifts.

Board meetings at Sunset Hills were more social than business-like and affairs of the school were incidentally discussed over refreshments. The chairman presided but Marion Koogler dominated.

From 1944 Mrs. McNay took over the directorship of the Institute and Mrs. Ellen Quillin served as assistant director. Although the Institute continued under the sponsorship of the San Antonio Art League, school board members found their functions were nominal, particularly in such matters as the selection of the teaching staff. They usually learned of school plans after they had been instituted by the director. Mrs. McNay left the task of placating the board members to the efficient Mrs. Quillin and continued to run things her own way.

Mrs. McNay changed her original plan to found a municipally operated museum to one privately administered for the public use. A board of seven persons, at least three of them men, named by her would receive her treasures in trust, be responsible for executing her plans for a nonprofit, perpetual museum and would serve without pay. The selection of the seven qualified persons was a source of concern to her and a subject she frequently discussed with Mrs. Quillin, who during Mrs. McNay's illness supervised school activities in addition to her other duties as business manager, superintendent, and peacemaker.

After extensive consideration and rejections and over a period of years, the field of prospective trustees was narrowed to seven trusted friends, each selected for a specific reason and, as Mrs. McNay said, "in each of whom I have entire con-

60

Entrance Hall, Marion Koogler McNay Art Institute

Marion Koogler McNay. "She had the everlasting beauty of a woman
like Katharine Cornell."

fidence." She selected: Mrs. Emily Brown, long active in the San Antonio Art League and the Art Institute and a woman of uncompromising integrity whose modesty and simplicity belied her own great personal wealth; Mrs. Ellen Quillin, whose selflessness and executive ability had been firmly established in the founding and developing of the city's Witte Museum; Mrs. Elsie McNay, who was thoroughly familiar with her plans, the collection, her wishes in the conversion and operation of the museum, and who had a knowledge of and appreciation for modern art; Mrs. Olivia Nolte, who had long served as chairman of the Witte Art School and who, as a bank director, was experienced in investments; Dr. Frederic G. Oppenheimer, who possessed both knowledge and love for art and whose generosity in sharing

his own collection was a matter of record; and Joseph H. Frost, president, and Robert C. Smith, vice-president of the Frost National Bank, each a personal friend as well as a financial adviser long familiar with her investments.

Marion Koogler's goal was to assemble a comprehensive collection of modern French art, illustrating its growth and development with examples by artists from Delacroix to Picasso and beyond. Fully aware of the gaps, she hastened to close as many as possible.

For example, she wanted a great Degas. But when Mr. Hatfield found one—*Two Dancers in Blue*—he also showed her the magnificent Cezanne *Portrait of Henri Gasquet*. Her "picture money" would not cover the cost of both and Mrs. McNay selected the Cezanne. On the other hand she had several Gauguins to which she added the now well-known *Portrait of the Artist With the Idol,* for which she paid $16,000. Recently when it was on loan to the Hatfield Galleries, a client said he would pay $275,000 for it if it could be bought which, of course, it could not be.

Mr. Hatfield frequently advised her to buy a large and important Renoir. But Renoir was represented in the Collection by a small *Gabrielle,* an early purchase from the Johnson Gallery. Rather than invest heavily in one painting, Mrs. McNay usually spread her expenditure over a selection of several small works in order to acquire examples by different artists. She did not judge the merits of a painting by its size but her choice, as a rule, was a small and intimate canvas. She was also aware of the limited scope of the walls of her house for displaying large canvases. The largest painting in the Collection is Dufy's *Golfe Juan,* $32\frac{3}{16}''$ x $39\frac{5}{8}''$.

Mrs. McNay frequently expressed the belief that a collector's primary concern was in the field of contemporary art. She felt it was obligatory that both private and public collectors give recognition to great artists of their own time and preserve their works for future generations rather than to delegate such responsibility to another age.

The completion of her collection consumed all her thoughts, her energy, and her available cash.

The Hatfields' last visit with Marion Koogler was a week before her death when they had a long conversation about paintings to be added to the collection.

"In spite of the fact that it is the most important collection of modern French art in Texas, there were many more paintings to be added," Mr. Hatfield said after her death. "Notably, it lacked a Delacroix, Corot, Manet, and Monet. She realized that although she had provided for future purchases in her will, permanent paintings would be added slowly. But special loan and traveling exhibitions in the interim

would hold the interest of the public and make the museum a vital force. She was a very wise woman and thoroughly versed in muscology and art affairs. Those who attain enduring greatness render lasting service and Marion Koogler McNay was one of these. The Collection speaks eloquently for the cooperation of collector and dealer over a period of sixteen years."

Ruth Hatfield, fourteen years after Mrs. McNay's death, said: "I believe she has rendered the greatest service to the city of any of its women citizens. She did it so quietly and with such devotion, that no one could ever say she had any thought of personal aggrandizement. She was simply a most intelligent and dedicated collector and one of the most knowledgeable in her own field of modern art. She had an innate feeling for art and the quality in art."

During her last illness, a number of Marion Koogler's oldest and dearest friends from El Dorado visited her hospital room, among them being the Kirkpatricks and Mrs. Gladys Teter Spencer. In the room when she died was an immense arrangement of deep red roses to which was attached the card of Ray Tack of Wichita, Kansas.

By a stranger-than-fiction twist, Marion Koogler's first sweetheart, the Catholic boy she did not marry, had reentered her life. The circumstances were later told by Ray Tack's daughter Mrs. Mary Kay Harrell of Wichita.

Ray Tack and his wife Mary had been pleasantly surprised to receive an invitation from Marion Koogler for the dedication of Charles Umlauf's *Crucifixion,* but were unable to attend. Later, after a fishing trip to Brownsville, Texas, the Tacks stopped in San Antonio and visited Mrs. McNay at Sunset Hills. It was the first time in forty-five years that Marion Koogler and Ray Tack had seen each other. Mary Tack and Marion Koogler became friends on sight and corresponded with each other until Mrs. Tack's death late in

Mrs. McNay and a new acquisition,
Paul Gauguin's *Portrait of the Artist with the Idol*

1949 in Rochester, New York. Daily, during Mrs. Tack's illness, Mrs. McNay telephoned to inquire about her condition.

The fall after Mary Tack's death, Ray Tack and his daughter accepted Mrs. McNay's invitation to visit Sunset Hills. Mrs. Harrell found her hostess "a perfectly charming and interesting person with a large capacity for warmth and affection and a marvelous way of encompassing people with her sincere devotion."

She was also generous, as Mrs. Harrell learned the following Christmas when Mrs. McNay sent "quite a large check" to be spent on toys for the Harrell children.

A short time before her death, Marion Koogler telephoned Ray Tack and asked him to come to San Antonio. But Ray Tack himself was ill at the time and the most he could do was to send a large bouquet of her favorite roses.

Some thought that had she lived Marion Koogler would have at long last married her high school sweetheart. Only seven days before she died she changed her will to include Ray Tack. The largest single cash bequest in her will—$25,000—was to him with the condition that it go to his daughter if he should predecease Mrs. McNay. Perhaps the gift was a sentimen-tal gesture in recognition of a lingering romance. Perhaps it was made in gratitude for Ray Tack's unknowingly directing her toward the peace of mind, personal happiness, and spiritual contentment for which she so long and futilely groped and found at last in the Church.

Mrs. McNay was not thought to be seriously ill and in fact was preparing to return to Sunset Hills when her weakened system collapsed under a virulent type of pneumonia. Elsie McNay and Mrs. Nancy DePew, a devoted friend of many years, were with her when she died April 13, 1950.

Marion Koogler had received Archbishop Lucey's consent to be buried in the cemetery next to Father Baque. She had asked his permission shortly after the dedication ceremony of Umlauf's *Crucifixion* and in granting it Archbishop Lucey expressed the hope that she would not soon take advantage of the privilege. She was buried in the cemetery of the Sisters of St. Anthony in a grave on one side of Father Baque. On the other side is the grave of Mother Theresa who died in 1951 at the age of eighty-one. Umlauf's *Crucifixion* casts its shadow across the three graves.

Plaque at left of entrance

IV. EPILOGUE

Marion Koogler McNay's final will, a legal marvel in clarity and completeness, is dated April 6, 1950. In addition to Ray Tack there were other individuals to whom she expressed appreciation and devotion by token bequests.

Esther and J. W. Kirkpatrick, of El Dorado, friends of long standing, were deeded one hundred and sixty acres of Butler County land and the leases thereon—the same acreage deeded to Marion Koogler by her father as a wedding gift in 1917. Esther Kirkpatrick received an antique blue enamel and diamond bracelet, a fur coat, Wedgwood dishes, and other china and crystal.

Ruth and Dalzell Hatfield were remembered with gifts of three antique French chairs, an Oriental rug, an antique wine cooler, and $10,000 to be applied to the purchase of a painting for their home. Ruth Hatfield also received a personal gift of a necklace, brooch, and bracelet of matching Russian garnets.

Mrs. Elsie McNay was given a furnished house, $5,000 in government bonds, a fur coat and a lyre-based game table; her son Don Denton McNay received $6,000 in government bonds.

The Susan B. Allen Memorial Hospital of El Dorado was willed $5,000. The same amount was given in trust to her cousin Mildred Hamilton to be used for the care of her mother (Mrs. McNay's aunt) Clara Lippincott.

Individual cash bequests included cousin Jessie Winkworth, $5,000; Alta Phillips, Marion, $3,000; Mrs. Gladys Teter Spencer of El Dorado and M. C. Armstrong, $2,500 each; Dr. and Mrs. E. V. DePew, San Antonio, $2,000; cousins Charles Koogler and Flora Poole, DeGraff, and Mrs. Ellen Quillin, $1,500 each; cousins Harry and Bernice Koogler and Helen Thatcher of DeGraff and Marion Thatcher Urick, Toledo, Ohio, Marie Esser, San Antonio, and Mildred Hamilton of Marion, $1,000 each; Georgia Maverick Harris, Evelyn Gerlack, and Eleanor Onderdonk of San Antonio and Marion Louise Thayer of Wichita, $500 each; and each employee, $100 for each full year of service.

The Marion Koogler McNay bequest to the Missionary Servants of Christ the Master and St. Anthony included: $15,000 to be applied to a shrine which "shall follow substantially the exterior of the Alamo" and be completed within five years after her death. (This bequest was forfeited due to delayed construction.) The Order also received an undivided one-third of Butler County real estate and oil and gas leases on it; five furnished rental houses; one-half of all bonds; two-thirds of all bank deposits; and one-half the proceeds from the sale of Marion, Ohio, and Pinellas County, Florida, real estate which was to be used for the construction of a Mother House.

To the illimitable public, Marion Koogler McNay gave her greatest possession—her incomparable perception of the visual arts. This gift was not contingent, as was Dr. Claribel Cone's art bequest to the people of Baltimore, on the improvement of the spirit of appreciation of modern art in San Antonio. Marion Koogler knew that appreciation was a result of exposure, and that her museum would provide the opportunity and privilege of visual communication.

The estate appraisal of the Collection, unrealistically modest, was $341,445, based on the approximate price the paintings would bring on the open market at the time of Mrs. McNay's death, less thirty percent which would have been the selling cost if sold through an auction or dealer.

The Frost National Bank of San Antonio received in trust, for the purpose of conveying title to a non-profit and perpetual corporation which would establish an art institute, the following: the 23.067 acres comprising Sunset Hills and all dwellings, furniture, and works of art on it; an undivided two-thirds of the Butler County real estate and leases; ten furnished houses off the Sunset Hills property; one-half of all bonds; one-third of all bank deposits; and one-half the proceeds of the Marion and Florida real estate.

The will assured an inviolate endowment fund which could be used only for reinvestment. Operating funds were limited to income from the endowment fund, rentals, and current income from bonds and stocks. A purchasing and building fund was possible when "income exceeding $20,000 over maintenance requirements for one year" had accumulated. The delayed fund was explained: "I have made extensive purchases of pictures in order to make my collection satisfactorily complete and representative. This was done to obviate the necessity for making any purchases of pictures in the immediate future."

To assure the continuing high standard of the Collection, all purchases and gifts were required to have the unanimous approval of the seven-member board, as well as the consent of the director of the Art Institute of Chicago ("mentioned first because of a diploma which I hold from the Art School"), the director of the Art Institute of Santa Barbara, California, and the head of the school of painting in the Fine Arts Department of The University of Texas.

Although the will gave trustees considerable latitude and discretion, some restrictions were imposed. Certain personal properties could be sold "but under no circumstances shall there be a public sale thereof at the premises" and rental real estate off the main property was saleable only with the unanimous consent of the trustees. It was Mrs. McNay's wish that neither the Kansas real estate nor leases be sold so long as oil is produced in paying quantities.

Property not subject to sale or disposal was specified: the Sunset Hills acreage; certain items of furniture (chests, *vargeña*, settles, tables, chairs, a Queen Anne desk and hunting table, vestment cupboards, dining room furniture, silver service, etc.); the "El Greco and my collection of modern art," *bultos, santos*, penitente crosses and crucifixes, ceremonial Indian rugs, Chimayo and Saltillo blankets, handwoven coverlets, costumes, textiles, and "my oxblood vase."

Her will provided for museum auxiliary membership but the Board of Trustees was prohibited from delegating to "such organization any of their duties in respect to management and control." Three lectures annually by men or women of recognized ability in the field of art were mandatory.

Conditions of admission and the continuation of the school were among decisions left to the board. There was a forfeiture clause for failure to carry out terms of the will by both the Missionary Servants and the museum. Title to the property of the organization failing to comply would pass to the other. If both failed, title to all the property would pass to the St. John Province, Order of Friars Minor, of Cincinnati, Ohio, to be used to establish an order in Texas.

Funds for the conversion of the home into a museum were to come from the first oil royalties received by the board after receiving title, and "because the nature of the changes to be made may be difficult to determine, I would be pleased

Nuestra Señora de Inmaculada, contemporary *bulto* by José Dolores
López, McNay Collection

Gallery of New Mexican Arts and Crafts, Marion Koogler McNay Art Institute

if the corporation would consult Dalzell and Ruth Hatfield . . . each of whom knows in detail my plan for utilizing this property as an art institute."

The Hatfields provided notes and drawings which itemized Mrs. McNay's instructions to them regarding final conversion plans. Numerous and minute details had been considered: lighting of paintings, location of electric outlets, removal of wall sconces and chandeliers; monk's cloth as a wall covering in some galleries and textured walls left intact in others; removal of specified walls, mainly in the bedroom area, to increase gallery sizes, and the sealing of fireplaces, certain windows and doors; location of reception desk and office, sculpture galleries, director's apartment, fireproof packing and storage rooms and closets, restrooms, and library; retention of the original porches, patios and terraces, and the stenciled ceilings and ceramic and glazed tiles. The Hatfields remembered her caution to repair a wall leakage in one room where dampness had seeped in and caused mildew on a number of watercolors including the beautiful Winslow Homer. Mrs. McNay's plan divided the house into connecting galleries, one of which she suggested be used for the display of her New Mexican *bultos* and *retablos*. She wanted the dining room to remain functional.

The Hatfields further explained:

70

Nuestra Señora del Carmel, New Mexican
bulto, McNay Collection

"Rarely in the history of the United States has a museum been started under such auspicious circumstances. Mrs. McNay realized, and often discussed with us, the fact that a museum is as great as the works of art it possesses, as important as the intelligence of its direction, and as influential as the service it renders. She was insistent that those changes she deemed necessary should be made in such

a way as to keep the character of the original architecture of her home. She did not want the museum she was founding to be a structure of cold walls, as she often said, but wanted it to be a place of beauty with the comforts and warmth of a home.

"She did not want visitors to be confronted and bound in by walls. Walls, she felt, should be broken by an occasional window through which a visitor inside could glimpse the sky and the landscaped gardens. To Marion, art and nature were one and she believed that paintings could be enjoyed more if seen in natural surroundings.

"Mrs. McNay wanted all changes to be made, the reconversion job completed, and the museum in perfect operating condition before opening it to the public or before any functions were held in it."

The Marion Koogler McNay Art Institute obtained its charter on September 23, 1952, and the first meeting of the board of trustees was held the next day. Dr. Frederic G. Oppenheimer was elected president; Mrs. Emily Brown, vice president; Mrs. Ellen Quillin, secretary, and Mrs. Elsie McNay, treasurer.

Dr. Oppenheimer was unable to attend meetings thereafter and Mrs. Brown served as president. Subsequently he resigned due to ill health and his nephew, Jesse H. Oppenheimer, a lawyer, was named by the trustees to fill his place. Mrs. Olivia Nolte also was unable to serve as a director and she was replaced by Mrs. Edgar Tobin, an art patron and collector. Joseph H. Frost died on July 31, 1956, and his nephew, Thomas C. Frost, Sr., then president of Frost National Bank, was elected to the vacancy.

John Palmer Leeper, then director of the Pasadena, California, Art Museum, was appointed director of the Marion Koogler McNay Art Institute on December 10, 1953.

The Museum property and holdings were released by the executor, William P. Mo-

Opening night scene, November 4, 1954. Mr. and Mrs. H. Lutcher Brown, left and right.
Center, Mrs. Jerry Bywaters, wife of the Director of the Dallas Museum of Fine Arts

loney, early in 1954, and reconversion began in May of that year.

The Trustees named the Frost National Bank to manage the investments of the perpetual endowment fund. That fund on August 26, 1954, before the museum opened, totalled $1,043,979.56. At the end of 1965, the income-producing endowment fund had increased to $2,913,781.30.

Dr. Koogler's oil wells, which Jessie Stratford had so accurately described many years before as unique, continued to pump. Their earnings bolstered the endowment fund by $213,370.99 in 1955 and in 1963 they pumped $98,282.41 into the fund.

Remodeling plans, closely following those outlined by Mrs. McNay to the Hatfields, were made by the original architects, Atlee B. and Robert M. Ayres. The exterior of the house, except for the closing of several windows and doors, was left intact.

Guests in central entrance hall, opening night

A fire-detection system, an elevator, central heating and cooling, and humidity control units were installed. Entrances to the grounds and walks leading to the buildings were lighted. Garden walks and patios were illuminated by concealed lights in large old olive jars. C. C. Fleming, landscape architect of Houston, redesigned the patio.

While interior work was in progress the Collection was stored in a downtown fireproof building. Watercolors were rematted on rag paper and many of them reframed. Sheldon Keck of New York, noted conservator of paintings, was engaged to do any necessary restoration of oil paintings.

A comprehensive catalogue of major examples of the Collection of one hundred and seventy-six paintings was prepared by Mr. Leeper, the director. Houston had only six modern paintings of the same quality, Dallas had two, Fort Worth had one, New

Orleans had none, and Kansas City had twelve.

Marion Koogler McNay's long-planned museum of modern art, the first and finest in the Southwest, became a reality on November 4, 1954.

The formal reception was a spectacular and glittering champagne first night. Hundreds of guests from all over the state attended and many national museums sent representatives. Many of the distinguished visitors had their first view of the Collection of the then little-known examples by French masters. In a few years the same paintings would be world famous.

On opening night, Marion Koogler's greatest treasures were on permanent display in the downstairs galleries. Upstairs was a loan exhibition of paintings and drawings by Pablo Picasso, the master of modern art. Appropriately, the first lec-

73

Board members Mrs. Ellen Quillin, left, and Mrs. Elsie McNay, right, at the opening night

turer was Mrs. McNay's friend, Daniel Catton Rich, at that time director of her beloved Art Institute of Chicago, whose topic was "That Art We Call Modern."

And thus was inaugurated Marion Koogler McNay's magnificent gift to San Antonio and to the world—truly a gem of a museum.

Indian Pueblo

Marion Koogler McNay

75

Navajo Weavers

Marion Koogler McNay

Indians Dancing

Marion Koogler McNay

77

Girl's Head

Seated Girl

Early drawings by Marion Koogler McNay, McNay Art Institute Collection

Henri Rousseau

Landscape with Milkmaids

79

Head of Christ   El Greco

Christ and Disciple   Georges Rouault

Paul Cezanne

Houses on the Hill

82

Golfe Juan   Raoul Dufy

83

Portrait of the Artist with the Idol   Paul Gauguin

84

Girl with Blue Eyes   Amedeo Modigliani

85

Portrait of Henri Gasquet   Paul Cezanne

Girl with Plumed Hat   Pablo Picasso

Dream Village   Marc Chagall

88

Vincent Van Gogh

Women Crossing the Fields

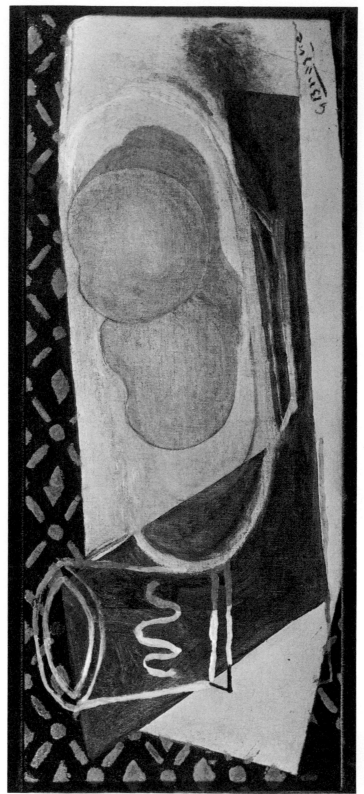

Still Life   Georges Braque

90

Hillside

91

The Cellist (Portrait of M. Serevitsch)   Chaim Soutine

92

The Red Blouse   Henri Matisse

94

Maurice Utrillo

Church of St. George de Didon

Camille Pissarro

Haymakers Resting

95

Guitar and Wine Glass   Pablo Picasso

96

Delfina Flores   Diego Rivera

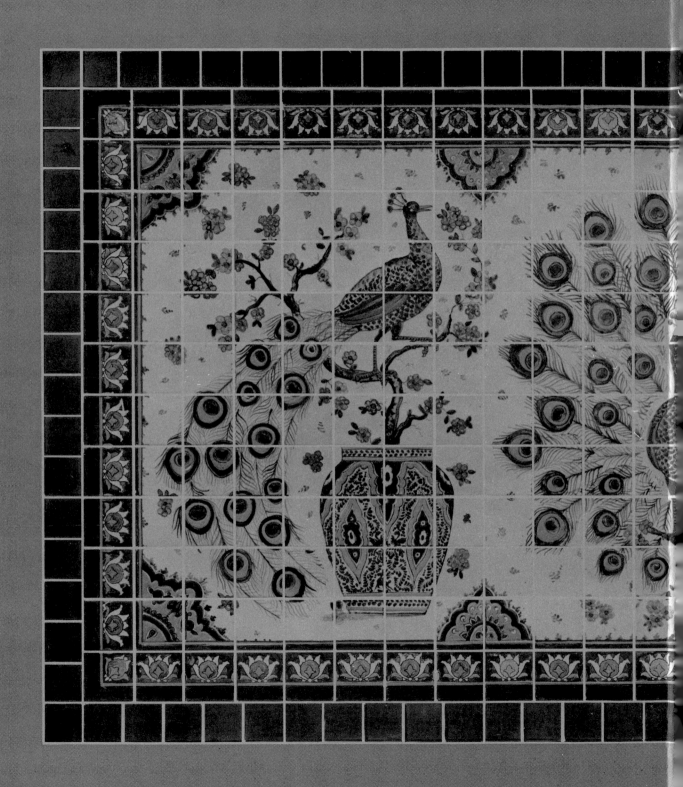